Your Child's Symptoms

Your Child's Symptoms

John Garwood, M.D., and Amanda Bennett

BERKLEY BOOKS, NEW YORK

YOUR CHILD'S SYMPTOMS

A Berkley Book / published by arrangement with
the authors

PRINTING HISTORY
Berkley trade paperback edition / June 1995

ISBN: 0-425-14734-7

BERKLEY®
Berkley Books are published by The Berkley Publishing Group,
200 Madison Avenue, New York, New York 10016.
BERKLEY and the "B" design
are trademarks belonging to Berkley Publishing Corporation.

PRINTED IN THE UNITED STATES OF AMERICA

10   9   8   7   6   5   4   3   2   1

ACKNOWLEDGMENTS

We would like to offer our thanks to the medical professionals who read this book: Katherine Grimm, M.D.; Barbara Hammond, R.N.; Robert Hammond, M.D.; Harry Harmon, M.D.; and Dana Holman, D.S.W. Their advice and suggestions provided invaluable help.

We would also like to thank the parents who read all or parts of the manuscript: Janet Bennett, Kathleen Christensen, Terence Foley, Leslie Garwood, Deborah Gobble, and Robin Weiss.

From Amanda Bennett—My thanks to my husband, Terence Foley, and to my son Terence Bennett Foley. I would also like to thank my mother, Janet Bennett, who, even without an M.D., is the best pediatrician I know.

From Dr. Garwood—My thanks to the hundreds of West Side families who make up my pediatric practice. It is the challenges they posed through their phone calls—at all times of the day and night—that make up the heart of this book. Special thanks also to my colleagues and friends at Mt. Sinai Hospital in New York, and especially to the Mt. Sinai pediatric emergency room staff. Their care of children and their teaching abilities are extraordinary.

I would also like to thank my wife, Leslie Garwood, and my children Sara, Daniel, and Evan, both for teaching me what the books and doctors couldn't, and for their patience during this project.

CONTENTS

SKIN
152

URINATION
170

INTRODUCTION

AMANDA:

Dr. John Garwood and I decided to write this book the night my son, Terry, threw up in my lap.

He was three years old, and had just started nursery school. He had been cranky that afternoon, but he certainly hadn't seemed sick. Now he was crying, and his temperature was close to 103°.

It was after nine P.M., so I tried to figure out what was wrong by myself. I reached for my stack of baby guides. With my sick child on my lap, I hastily paged through first one and then another of the guides. It was frustrating. For one thing, it wasn't easy to find anything on vomiting alone. Instead, I had to guess at a diagnosis myself and then take an anxious journey through descriptions of various diseases and causes to see whether the symptoms matched. It was an arduous task. One medical guide I checked had nineteen different entries on vomiting, which required me to page back and forth through descriptions of such topics as intussusception, gastroesophageal reflux, Reyes' Syndrome and intestinal obstructions.

Meanwhile, my husband had taken charge, and was busy feeding little Terry a cup of milk. Up it came. I simply *had* to call the doctor.

When Dr. John answered his emergency beeper, I realized there was something strange going on. Nothing he asked me had anything to do with anything I had read in my pediatric guides.

"How's he acting?" was one of his first questions. That was odd. Why did he want to know that? None of the books had been interested in the fact that, although my child was whimpering, he was sitting up watching a Sesame Street tape.

"What has he eaten today? What did he just eat before he vomited? Can he touch his chin to his chest? Does he seem like he has a stiff neck? What's going on at his school? Will he drink water?" All the questions were different ones than I expected.

A few more questions and Dr. John made his diagnosis: My son had a stomach virus. Deep in my heart, I had known that all along. I knew that there had been other cases at school. But what I really wanted was reassurance that there wasn't anything more serious afoot.

Dr. John gave me that reassurance. I had to watch Terry carefully, of course. But as long as he was sitting up, and willing to drink liquids, there was nothing much to be done but to wait it out.

Dr. John also made a few helpful suggestions. About that cup of milk, for example. We had been trying to soothe little Terry's stomach, but we had actually been making the problem worse, because little tummies sensitive from just having thrown up have a hard time with milk—and will often just throw it right back up again. I switched to water.

Very quickly, Terry got better, and Dr. John and I decided to write this book together. We realized there was nothing like it available for parents today. We wanted a book that talked to parents the way pediatricians talk to parents.

Certainly there are plenty of medical guides—plenty of really good ones. But no matter how user-friendly they try to be, these guides don't address symptoms the way parents see those symptoms. Instead, they force parents to wade through descriptions of one condition after another in search of the symptoms that match most closely. My experience wasn't at all unusual. One medical guide offers one hundred and seven page references to check for possible causes of crying. Another forces parents to turn to fourteen different places to reassure themselves about their child's cough, and to find out what to do about it. By the end of a journey like that, it's easy for a parent to become confused—or terrified.

Dr. John and I wanted a book for parents anxious about the health of their children that would be as warm and reassuring as the pediatrician's voice on the other end of the phone. *Your Child's Symptoms* addresses the childhood symptoms that a parent sees— exactly the way the parent sees them, and exactly the way the pediatrician in daily practice hears them.

Think of why most parents call pediatricians: They call because their child is vomiting. They call because their child is feverish. They call about a cough that goes on and on, or about an infant who won't stop crying. They want to know what is causing this symptom. Is it serious? When will it go away? What can I do to help my child?

DR. JOHN:

For twenty years I've been on the other side of calls like Amanda's. For twenty years, no matter what time of day or night, I've tried to talk worried parents through their fears for their children— sometimes with my own family staring me down from across the dinner table, wondering if this parade of calls would ever end.

The telephone is at the heart of my practice, as it is with many busy pediatricians. It is over the telephone that I deal with all sorts of problems, both those they teach you about in medical school, and those whose solutions pediatricians learn only through years of practice.

This book grew out of these telephone calls. It isn't a comprehensive diagnostic manual, nor an exhaustive medical dictionary. It isn't intended to substitute for any of the excellent medical guides already available. Rather, it is a book that I hope will be fun to read because it sounds the way I do on the phone: chatty, colloquial, and full of useful advice—but not stinting on humor either.

Your Child's Symptoms is logically organized and easy to read. Parents will be able to turn to the symptom that most closely matches their child's—a rash, a headache, diarrhea—and follow a discussion of that symptom conducted in the same methodical, orderly fashion that their pediatrician would follow. Under the section on *Coughing,* for example, the parents will be guided through a series of questions and observations: Where is the location of the problem? Does the cough seem to be coming from the chest or the throat? How long has it lasted? What other symptoms, like a runny nose or a high fever, has the parent seen? What does the cough sound like? Is there a history of asthma in the family, or of pneumonia?

This isn't just a sterile recitation of medical facts, however, but a discussion—the kind of a discussion a parent would have with a trusted family physician. You will find the book filled with surprising and useful insight. Such as: What is the one thing parents almost never ask themselves about a sick child that pediatricians always do? Why is your child's cough hazardous to your bathroom wallpaper? How does where you spent your last vacation affect your doctor's diagnosis of your child's illness? What is one of the most feared—and least common—childhood ailments? What is the first thing doctors suggest be done to help make a feverish child more comfortable—and why do parents hate to do it?

At the same time I realized that parents needed a book that spoke directly to the very real fears that lead them to call the pediatrician. I realized that the questions Amanda was asking me masked her underlying fears that Terry had some serious, life-threatening illness. I knew, the way existing child health guides don't, that when parents call late at night about a headache, they aren't necessarily only concerned about whether the child is suffering from a sinus infection or is just overtired. Parents naturally worry about the worst: things like brain tumors and meningitis.

What's more, as a doctor, I knew that symptoms that meant one thing to me as a medical professional often had much scarier implications for parents. In adults chest pains, or blood in the stools can signal a life-threatening condition; in children it usually doesn't.

Still, most parents often are more anxious than they ought to be, because they unconsciously associate their childrens' symptoms with their own.

But kids are not little adults. Children have different symptoms. They have different diseases. They react differently to medication. For the most part, childrens' symptoms are far less likely to presage serious medical conditions than adults' symptoms do. There are several things chest pains can mean in a child—but heart attack is almost never one of them.

The organization of this book unlocks the happy fact that most kids are basically healthy. While this book will give guidance about those signs and symptoms that clearly indicate a quick trip to the hospital or at least a late-night phone call to the pediatrician, the focus will be on reassurance.

Our children are infinitely precious. If there is any chance, however slight, of real trouble, we fret. But we both wanted to write a book to put those fears in context, as any good pediatrician will. We wrote a book that gives solid advice for identifying these dangerous conditions. But at the same time our book talks about the other illnesses, the more common viruses and winter coughs and ear infections that actually cause the vast majority of problems in children.

What's more, this book will give parents real assistance in overcoming the helplessness many feel when confronted with an uncomfortable child. In each section, this book will offer instructions on do-it-yourself care to help relieve the child's symptoms and to prevent complications. And it distinguishes clearly between the illnesses of infants and the illnesses of older children. There are many conditions that are much more serious in infants under six months of age than in older children. Things like fever, vomiting, and diarrhea need much closer attention when the child is six months or under. Our book separates the two groups into different sections so that parents of infants will pay closer attention to potentially worrisome symptoms while parents of older kids will be more easily reassured.

Of course no book can be a real substitute for your own pediatrician. Use this book as a guide, but follow your own instincts.

If you have any questions at all, call your pediatrician anyway. Your doctor knows best about your child.

This book begins with a discussion of Fever. That's partly because fever is such a common childhood symptom. It's also because it's one of the symptoms that is least understood by parents. It's also a symptom that occurs along with many other symptoms. The more parents understand about fevers and the way pediatricians look at them, the more they will be prepared to understand their own child's illness.

After that, each chapter contains a basic discussion of the major symptom—like Coughs, Vomiting, Diarrhea—and of the other kinds of symptoms that can accompany the major one. Within most chapters, there are seven sections:

- ❖ **Overview:** A basic discussion of the symptom and its likely causes
- ❖ **Your Child Under Six Months:** The special problems and issues of sick babies
- ❖ **Checklist:** A quick digest of the material in the basic discussion for easy reference
- ❖ **Treatment:** Suggestions for home care of your sick child
- ❖ **Shall I Wake the Doctor?:** A quick guide to the serious symptoms that always require immediate attention
- ❖ **Can He/She Go Back to School?:** How to tell if your child is well enough to resume normal activities
- ❖ **Ask Dr. John:** Informal questions

Because we know that kids come in two varieties, we've split the use of pronouns: Half the chapters use "he" and half use "she."

We hope you find this book valuable, reassuring and easy to use.

AMANDA BENNETT   JOHN GARWOOD, M.D.

Your Child's Symptoms

FEVER

Here's a story one father told me recently about a frenzied dash to the hospital that he made with his feverish son. When the child's temperature hit 104°, and the boy started acting delirious, the parents decided they couldn't wait. Even though it was late at night, the hospital was a half hour drive away, and there was a West Virginia blizzard raging outside, they bundled the boy into the car for the trip to the emergency room. It was a hair-raising ride. To make matters worse, a loose link on the snow tires banged against the underside of the car at every revolution, jarring their nerves even further.

The parents were frantic—until they reached the hospital. Then up popped their son, demanding his bottle. His nose was running and his face was flushed, but his fever was down, his good humor was restored, and he was obviously ready for some serious play. Today the little boy in question is a healthy strapping young man in his twenties, apparently none the worse for the incident.

And so it goes with most feverish children. Fever is one of the most common symptoms parents and pediatricians confront, and it certainly is among the scariest. The reaction of this little boy's parents was very typical of parents whose children suddenly run high fevers. They wanted help, and they wanted it right away. Their concern is perfectly understandable: It's distressing to pick the baby up from his nap only to discover he is burning hot, or to watch the mercury on the fever thermometer shoot up to 105°. In adults, high fevers do indeed send up warning flags. An internist is likely to be alarmed by a call from an adult with a 105° fever, since adults don't usually run fevers that high unless something serious—like pneumonia or a bad infection—is in full swing. But for a pediatrician, such a call is almost routine. After checking for certain other symptoms that might, in fact, indicate a more serious condition, the doctor can often give enough helpful advice over the phone to help parents through the crisis. In a majority of cases, a trip to the office isn't even necessary.

High fever can mean serious illness in adults, but in children it very seldom does. Fever, even very high fever, usually signals nothing more than a child's normal response to the onset of a non-threatening viral illness. The child may be uncomfortable and the parents may be anxious, but in fact the fever is just the baby's body doing its job.

Remember: What we learned as normal temperature—98.6—is only a guideline. Average temperatures for children and adults do vary, as do children's responses to disease. Parents often get very familiar with their own children's patterns, which even in one family may vary greatly. One child may regularly have temperatures that bounce up to 105°, while another may seldom top 102°. Temperatures in children, as in adults, tend to be higher in the afternoon or evening.

Don't misunderstand me, we pediatricians always take fevers seriously, and so should you. Later on, I will describe certain things you might see in your baby or child that, if accompanied by a fever, would certainly warrant a quick call to the doctor, or even a trip to the emergency room. But the thing you should remember is that it will be a combination of symptoms seen *in conjunction* with a fever, and not the fever itself, that sets off my alarm and should set off yours too.

That said, let me state one important principle to remember as you observe your feverish child: **It is simply not true that a**

higher fever means a sicker kid. Many parents figure that a temperature of 103° is more worrisome than one of 101°, and therefore 105° must certainly mean the child's condition is graver than the last time he ran a 104° fever. This assumption is understandable but incorrect.

Like the father in my example, 104° seems to be the level of fever parents can tolerate in their child before they need reassurance. As I flip through my notebook recording recent calls from concerned parents, I find that page after page lists kids whose temperatures have just topped 104°. At this level, I guess parents figure things have really taken a turn for the worse.

But that just isn't the case. The body's temperature is controlled by the brain, and is affected by certain products that germs release into the bloodstream. For some reason, just as children's sleeping patterns are quite different from those of adults, this temperature control mechanism is quite different too. Young children's temperature swings are far more volatile and far more extreme, probably because of some neurological set point that shifts as the child grows older. Since fever is one way of combating disease, this mechanism was probably especially useful before we had antibiotics to help very young children fight off infection.

This situation changes gradually over time, with the child's fever patterns beginning to more closely resemble those of an adult's at about school age. Still, even after the age of five and six, many children will continue to run high fevers that are no cause for alarm.

I will let you in on a little professional secret. Some pediatricians in private practice don't worry about the child's fever *by itself* until the mercury hits 105°. Below that level, if the other warning signs of a more serious condition are not present, the chances are great that the child is simply responding to a viral illness. That level of fever warrants a phone call. What's more, I'll usually want to at least take a look at a child whose fever has reached 106°. At 106° and above, I feel there is enough risk that the fever itself is caused by a more serious problem. So I feel it is wise to have the child come to my office to be examined. Below that level, however, I usually feel comfortable trying to figure out the problem over the phone.

WHAT IS A FEVER?

By mouth: Over 99.5 degrees
By armpit: Over 98.6 degrees
Rectally: Over 100.4 degrees

Because normal temperatures vary from person to person, you should try to establish your child's own baseline temperature. Take his temperature on several days when he is not sick. I will often get calls from parents who say that, although their child seems to have recovered from his illness, his temperature remains stubbornly elevated. I suggest they wait a day or two and try again. Sure enough, the temperature is still up there, and we conclude that this is a child who simply runs hot normally.

THE TWO BIG FEARS

When I talk with parents about their child's fever, either in person or over the phone, there are always two unspoken topics hovering in the air. Most parents are often too embarrassed, too frightened or too inhibited to ask about these things right out. But the questions torment them nonetheless. I will address them right now.

The two topics are **meningitis** and **brain damage.**

In my experience, most parents worry about their child's fever because of an almost visceral fear that he has contracted meningitis and will die, or that if the fever is left unchecked, he will suffer some grave mental harm. This fear is prevalent even among experienced parents who have lived through several fevers, and who know intellectually that the fever is probably caused by a virus. In the case of meningitis, most parents probably have some experience in the back of their minds that feeds this fear. Probably all of us have heard stories about a child who did contract meningitis and die. Or perhaps there are some newspaper accounts of outbreaks of meningitis that we can recall. As for fever causing brain damage, parents perhaps unconsciously recall stories of children never fully recovering from their fevers. The brain and a person's mental functioning are very sensitive, very emotional topics for everyone. So it's only natural that such stories have such power over parents.

Let me tell you how I, and other pediatricians, consider these two subjects.

Meningitis is certainly one of the first things that I too consider when a parent calls to consult me about his child's fever. Because it is such a serious disease, and does carry the possibility of being fatal, I want to check immediately for any signs that meningitis might be the cause. But let me stress here that my goal is largely to *rule out* meningitis.

The key to understanding meningitis is to realize that meningitis almost never presents itself only as a fever. There are almost always other symptoms that can be clearly observed. Here are the questions I ask parents in order to test whether we should suspect meningitis. Ask yourself these questions. But be aware: If you have the slightest doubt as to the answers you give yourself, by all means call your pediatrician and discuss the situation with him or her. It is much better to be safe than sorry. But the chances are, you too will discover that something far more benign is at work.

Here's what to look for:

- ❖ Does your child appear to have a severe headache along with the fever? In an older child, there won't be much question of this. The child who can talk will tell you.
- ❖ Does the child appear limp? Children of walking age who have meningitis will often be unable to walk or to stand up.
- ❖ Can the child touch his chin to his chest? Meningitis causes a very severe stiff neck, and children suffering from it won't be able to bend their heads far enough forward to touch their chests. **Remember: This is different from an ordinary stiff neck, in which the child may complain of stiffness when rotating the head from side to side.**
- ❖ Is the child vomiting repeatedly? Again, children with the

flu often complain of headache and vomiting. With meningitis, the vomiting usually will be *repeated*.

If you see these symptoms together, along with a fever (whether or not it's a high fever), call your physician immediately. I would stress here though, that most of these symptoms need to be present. Many children who are simply suffering from a viral infection will have a fever, vomiting and a mild headache. If you aren't sure, call the doctor. If nothing else, you will feel better for the extra reassurance.

But let me assure you that statistics are very much on your side. In the first place, meningitis these days is a very rare condition. During my days in medical school, I saw cases of meningitis. As an emergency room physician, I have helped diagnose and treat children with meningitis. And I have consulted with other doctors who have had children in their practice contract the disease. Just this winter, a case of meningitis at an exclusive private school sent shivers through the local community of parents. In my entire twenty-five years of private practice I have seen thousands of children from every type of family background and every socioeconomic class, from the very richest to the most impoverished, but I have only diagnosed a handful of cases of meningitis among my own patients.

In the last few years especially, the widespread use of the Hib vaccine has greatly reduced one of the major underlying bacterial causes of meningitis. (It is now recommended that children receive this vaccine beginning at two months of age.) If I haven't found any of the other symptoms of meningitis in a feverish child, I usually don't worry too much after I hang up the phone. If I've found out that the child has had his or her Hib vaccine, as is true for more and more very young children, I can truly sleep easily that night.

When we pediatricians worry about the effect of a high fever on the body, including the brain, we worry about more than just the height the temperature attains. We must also know what caused it and how the fever responds to our efforts to bring it down. Later in this chapter I will suggest ways to reduce a child's fever. If a fever over 106° Fahrenheit taken rectally will not respond to these efforts, that is a real cause for alarm. This kind of fever is most often seen in conjunction with heat stroke (a condition I will also discuss later), during surgery, with meningitis and with blood infections.

In the vast majority of other cases, however, you will find that your child's fever will respond quite nicely to the treatments I will suggest.

OUR SINGLE BIGGEST GUIDE: BEHAVIOR

While parents are likely to focus on the fever itself, pediatricians want to look at the whole child. While parents may not appreciate the analogy, children, especially very young children, are a lot like animals. When they can't talk, or can't describe their symptoms clearly, we fall back on watching their behavior. In fact, behavior is an extremely accurate sign of a child's underlying condition. While most parents focus on the things about their children that aren't working, a pediatrician is likely to be more concerned about the parts that are. A very sick child simply acts very sick. If after basic treatment for the fever, the child begins acting more normally, it's less likely he has something serious. So watch your child and ask yourself:

❖ What is he doing right now?
❖ Will he take his bottle?
❖ Will he eat?
❖ What is he wearing?
❖ When we begin to lower his temperature, does he perk up?

Whatever the mercury says, if your child is careening through the house, snatching toys from his younger brother, pulling down his favorite fire truck, demanding juice, cookies, cereal and popsicles and clamoring to watch more TV, he probably isn't very sick.

Still, a child with a very high fever isn't likely to be that cheerful. A child with a high fever is likely to be an unhappy little creature—whining, clinging and showing little interest in food or toys. The key lies in watching to see whether or not that unhappy behavior persists for more than, say, an hour after you've begun to use the methods I suggest to bring his fever down.

In general, once the child's temperature has been brought down under 101°, he should look, act and feel much better. If your child then perks up, asks for his bottle and demands to be taken back to the park, the chances are that his condition isn't serious.

In that case, I would let him do pretty much what he wants. The only caution would be against letting him play too actively, since motion can increase the fever again. If possible, try to keep him involved in quieter activities like reading books or watching TV.

THE MOST USUAL CAUSES OF FEVER

Here's how the typical call into my office might sound:

Doctor, my child went down to take his afternoon nap and he was feeling perfectly fine. He had a little runny nose, but otherwise he was no different than usual. He ate okay, went out to the park, came home at the usual time and went down to sleep. But when he woke up, I picked him up and he was burning up. It was like he was on fire. I took his temperature rectally, and it's 104.5°.

When pediatricians get phone calls like that, most of us will begin a methodical examination of the child's condition. Here's how I would start:

- ❖ Does the child have a runny nose?
- ❖ Is he complaining that his arms and legs ache?
- ❖ Does he have a cough that started recently?
- ❖ Has he vomited recently?
- ❖ How about diarrhea?
- ❖ Does he have a spotted rash?

I would start with those questions because they would lead me to the most likely cause of the child's fever: a **viral infection.** There are basically two kinds of viral illnesses that affect children. One— the kind that comes with coughing and runny noses—we usually see more in the winter time. The other—that affects the stomach and intestines—is more of a summertime ailment and usually begins to break out in the late spring. Both types can also cause a rash.

During the late fall and winter, if the child who, has been previously well (except for a runny nose or a minor cough) suddenly develops a high fever, I would suspect a viral illness. If the child seems whiny and complains of body aches, that's further evidence. A child in the throes of a viral infection is likely to be cranky and clingy and to lose interest in play and in his bottle or his toys.

In the summertime, we are more likely to see a fever that again begins in a relatively healthy child, but instead of a cough and a runny nose, is accompanied by vomiting and diarrhea. Every spring my phone rings off the hook with this type of virus. For that reason we sometimes call these summer viruses. There is a family of viruses called **enteric viruses** which flourish in the intestinal tract. One is called the **Coxsackie virus** (named after a town in New York state, midway between New York City and Albany, where the virus was first identified). The second is called **echo virus.** These are the common viruses of the spring and summer. It doesn't much matter which one your child gets—indeed it would take some sophisticated laboratory work to figure it out—because with one exception, both viruses act pretty much the same.

That one exception is a characteristic rash that comes with some types of Coxsackie viruses. Kids will show up with a high fever and spots on the soles of their feet, the palms of their hands and around their mouths. We call this hand-foot-mouth syndrome. All that rash does is help us confirm our diagnosis of the virus. It isn't dangerous to the child, although it can be uncomfortable.

BE ALERT FOR THESE SYMPTOMS

Children do get more serious ailments that will require a doctor's attention. So watch carefully for the following signs:

❖ Is the child hoarse?
❖ Is he trying to put his fist down his throat?
❖ Is he having trouble talking or swallowing?
❖ Has he been coughing for a few days?
❖ Does his breathing seem labored?
❖ Is he tugging on his ear, or complaining that his ears hurt?
❖ Is there a greenish discharge from his nose?
❖ Does he continue to act listless or uncomfortable after you've brought the fever down?

A child who is hoarse when he talks, or who appears to be having trouble talking or swallowing may have a **strep throat** or **pharyngitis.** (Pharyngitis means an inflammation anywhere along the throat.) A very young child who can't talk will often indicate a sore throat by trying to jam his fist down his throat—presumably in an effort to get to the place that hurts. Sore throats are usually just inflammations, but a child with a sore throat and fever ought to be examined by a doctor. That's because of the possibility of strep throat—a bacterial infection that can, if left untreated, lead to a more serious condition, known as rheumatic fever, which includes damage to the heart muscle. If you suspect from observing your child's behavior that he might have a sore throat along with his fever, check with your doctor. He or she may recommend an office visit to determine whether the sore throat is strep, or just another symptom of a viral infection.

Children who have been coughing for more than a couple of days, or who appear to be in some distress when breathing, or who complain of chest pain along with their fever may be exhibiting symptoms of **pneumonia.** [see: Coughing] Again, a phone call to the doctor is advised.

A fever combined with complaints of ear pain, or in a younger child, with swatting at or tugging at the ear, may mean that the child has an **ear infection.** [see: Ears] This is a common condition, but nonetheless should be confirmed by a doctor and treated with antibiotics.

A child with a fever and greenish, or greenish-yellow discharge from his nose should be examined for possible **sinus infection.**

(see: Noses) Remember, though, that this discharge will definitely have a strong-color and be rather thick—quite unlike the watery, grayish or milky-colored discharge of a child with a normal garden-variety cold.

HEAT STROKE

A fever in the summer, after a child has been playing outdoors for a long time, is a sign of a completely different and very serious condition called **heat stroke.** Fortunately it is very rare and very preventable. Heat stroke is caused when the body's mechanism to control temperature is reset so that the body doesn't recognize the high fever. Thus it doesn't do the things it ordinarily does by itself to bring the temperature down. The body gets stuck with this high fever and considers it normal.

This happens when the body is exposed to long periods of high heat, usually combined with dehydration. It most often occurs during unsupervised athletic situations where kids, say, play tennis all day long in the hot sun and don't drink enough. A child with heat stroke is a very sick child. So be alert in the summertime for a very high fever, and perhaps a loss of consciousness. If you see something like that happening, *get the child to the emergency room immediately* where special cooling pads can be used to bring the body temperature down.

In the meantime, it's helpful to remember that heat stroke is a completely preventable condition. Children, especially very young children, should drink plenty of fluids in hot weather, and not overdo it by running about for hours without a break when the outdoor temperature is high.

THE PERSISTENT, LOW-GRADE FEVER

Fevers in young children are so common, and by themselves mean so little, that some physicians think parents shouldn't even bother themselves with checking a child's temperature at all.

I disagree. There are some cases where a low-grade temperature, documented over a period of days, can in itself indicate problems. Ask yourself this question: Has he had a persistent low-grade fever of 100° or more for three days or more?

In such a case, I would call your physician for an evaluation. A low-grade fever that won't go away might be signalling some underlying condition that isn't yet serious enough to cause other symptoms. Some possible candidates: **rheumatoid arthritis,** a chronic condition that requires evaluation and treatment; **urinary tract infections,** (see: Urination) which in adults can be quite painful, but in children who can't accurately report their discomfort can sometimes pass unnoticed.

FEVER CONVULSIONS

A fever convulsion is one of the scarier events a parent can face and requires prompt medical attention. Fortunately, such convulsions almost always pass quickly and leave the child feeling none the worse. Still, you should call the doctor and prepare for a quick trip to his or her office, or to the emergency room.

Fever convulsions occur in some children with high fevers, or whose temperatures are rapidly rising. There are some children we know who are prone to fever seizures because of earlier brain damage or some developmental abnormality. But in otherwise normal children, we aren't sure exactly why they have an episode or two of fever seizures. The major factor seems to be not the height of the temperature, but how quickly it is rising. It seems that a rapidly-rising temperature can short-circuit some kids' ability to cope, leading to seizures.

Generally, what a parent will see will be very frightening. The child may experience a general rhythmic shaking of his arms and legs. He may vomit or drool, and may pass urine or feces. The most important thing is to position the child so the he doesn't choke on his vomit. Turn him on his side and stay calm.

Often the seizure is short, sometimes as short as 30 seconds. Indeed, by the time you have finished dialing the doctor, the child may be past the worst of the seizure. Still, complete your call and consult with your physician. If he or she isn't available, take the child to the nearest emergency room. Even after the seizure has passed, the child should be examined, most importantly to rule out meningitis which can sometimes announce itself with a high fever and a seizure. But most parents can be assured that, frightening as the event appears, in the vast majority of cases the episode will produce no lasting harm.

WHEN THE FEVER COMES SECOND

There are many other medical conditions that are accompanied by fever, but where the fever isn't necessarily the main symptom. Here are a few of the major situations. For more information about these conditions, consult the bracketed section I refer to.

YOUR CHILD UNDER SIX MONTHS

In an infant, we define fever as anything over 100.4° rectally. In very young children, especially those under two months of age, we take fevers very seriously. In fact, it's one of the reasons we tell parents to have thermometers on hand when they bring their baby home from the hospital. The reason is that in a young child a fever is much more likely to herald a serious illness than it is even in a child just a few months older. Bacterial infections are much more common in infants than they are in older children. What's more, it's more likely that infants will have serious illnesses that have no other symptoms besides a fever.

Because the clues that we use in diagnosing older kids—their behavior and eating patterns—are so much more difficult to read in infants, I want parents to call me immediately if their newborn shows any sign of fever. In a two-month-old child, you can't use the same technique you do with her older brother of simply giving her acetaminophen and watching to see if she improves. It's just too likely that she might become seriously ill quickly. Call your doctor right away. He or she may want to see your child immediately.

Fortunately, such attention is only required for a very brief period. At even three months of age children are much more robust and much less susceptible to the kinds of bacterial infections that can cause problems in young babies. Their immune systems are more developed and ready to fight off any infections they might contract.

So to repeat: In a child under two months of age, a fever is a fever. It doesn't matter how high it is. If the thermometer reads over 100.4°, call your doctor. Chances are your baby just has a virus. But we want to be especially careful with your little one.

CHECKLIST

FEVER WITH:

ABDOMINAL PAIN: You will most likely have noticed the abdominal pain first, or vomiting or some diarrhea. Most likely, the child has a simple **viral infection** [see: Diarrhea]. But there is also a possibility of **appendicitis** [see: Pain]. In appendicitis, fever isn't always present, and when it is, it may be low-grade.

URINARY TROUBLES: Kids can develop a fever at any time during a **urinary tract infection** [see: Urination]. The kids will complain first that it hurts when they make peepee, and the urine may be foul-smelling and frequent.

SEVERE HEADACHE, LIMPNESS, POSSIBLE INABILITY TO WALK, STIFF NECK, INABILITY TO TOUCH THE CHIN TO THE CHEST, REPEATED VOMITING: Suspect **meningitis** and call the pediatrician at once. The doctor will either want to see the child in his or her office, or, if the symptoms related over the phone seem serious enough, may send the child directly to the emergency room.

HOARSENESS, TROUBLE TALKING OR SWALLOWING OR, IN VERY YOUNG CHILDREN, ATTEMPTS TO PUT HIS FIST DOWN HIS THROAT: Suspect a sore throat and call the pediatrician at once. The doctor should test for **strep throat,** which should be treated with antibiotics.

DIFFICULTY SWALLOWING: A kid with viral croup should be yelling and hollering and able to suck on his bottle. If he can't talk, suck or swallow, suspect **epiglottitis** [see: Cough] and call the physician or head for the emergency room at once.

PERSISTENT COUGHING, COMPLAINTS OF CHEST PAINS OR BREATHING THAT SEEMS LABORED OR RAPID: Suspect **pneumonia** [see: Cough] and call the pediatrician at once.

COMPLAINTS OF EAR PAIN OR, IN YOUNGER CHILDREN, PERSISTENT TUGGING ON THE EAR: Suspect an **ear infection** [see: Ears]. This condition is common, but should be confirmed and treated with antibiotics.

CONTINUED LISTLESSNESS AFTER THE FEVER HAS BEEN BROUGHT DOWN WITH ACETAMINOPHEN OR COOL BATHS: Most likely the child is still suffering from a **viral infection.** Still, check with your doctor to discuss the possibilities of other more serious illnesses.

RUNNY NOSE, COUGHING AND CRANKINESS, ESPECIALLY IN THE WINTER: Suspect a **viral infection.** Follow instructions on "How to Bring a Fever Down." If listlessness and crankiness persist even after the fever is controlled, call your pediatrician.

VOMITING, DIARRHEA AND CRANKINESS, ESPECIALLY IN THE SUMMER: Suspect a **viral infection** [see: Vomitting, Diarrhea]. Follow instructions on "How to Bring a Fever Down." If listlessness and crankiness persist even after the fever is controlled, call your pediatrician.

GREENISH NASAL DISCHARGE: Suspect **sinus infection** [see: Noses]. The child should be examined and possibly treated with antibiotics.

TREATMENT

Sometimes parents ask me whether they should even bother bringing a child's fever down, since fever is the body's way of fighting infection. I think they should. One major reason is that the child's response to efforts to cool him off is a major tool for diagnosis. Once the fever is reduced, we can look at behavior. What's more, a feverish child is often a very unhappy child. Reducing the fever makes the child more comfortable.

There are four basic ways to bring down a fever, and I usually recommend that parents use all four of them since they complement each other. Here's the order in which I would recommend them:

1) *Undress a fever.* This is the step most parents find difficult to do. Often when I ask parents what their feverish child is wearing, they will tell me that they have just bundled the tot up in sweaters and blankets. This urge to bundle up a fever is probably left over from the days before central heating when both children and adults ran a serious risk of chill, even indoors. Or it might be left over from the days before antibiotics when one method of treating bacterial infections was to bundle up the child in hopes of driving the fever up and burning the infection off. These days, though, it's just the wrong thing to do, since bundling does in fact drive the fever up. Instead, I recommend that parents immediately undress their child. Let him run about in a diaper and t-shirt. Parents balk at this, but it's still a very effective treatment.

2) *Use acetaminophen.* This is the active ingredient in any of the over-the-counter pain relievers like Tylenol, Panadol, Liquiprin, and Tempra. Use the children's version and follow the recom-

mended dose. *Do not use aspirin* to reduce a child's fever, since aspirin can increase a child's chances of contracting Reyes' Syndrome, a serious neurological disorder. I recommend doing this step soon after step one, because the medication takes between 40 minutes and an hour to become effective. Ibuprofen, which is the active ingredient of such medications as Advil and Motrin can also be used.

3) *Use sponge baths.* This is one old-fashioned technique that really works. Put the child in the bathtub and sponge him off with tepid water. Don't use cold water, because that might cause shivering, which is actually the body's way of warming itself up again. And don't use alcohol. Forget whatever you may have heard about its effectiveness in cooling down patients in hospitals. Research hasn't shown that it works any better than water. What's more, children breathing in the fumes of alcohol can and actually do become intoxicated from breathing them.

4) *Give fluids.* I put this step last simply because many feverish children will refuse a bottle. If yours will drink readily, be sure and give him all he wants. I often find, though, that we need to drop the temperature a bit using the above three methods before children will willingly drink enough to make a difference. Feverish children need much more liquid than usual, since the elevated temperature causes them to burn off water more quickly in the form of perspiration.

Some parents complain that even after following these steps their child's fever remains stubbornly in the 102° range. I remind them that if they hadn't begun to treat the fever, it probably would have risen in that time to spike around 104° or 105°. What the parents have done is contained the fever. A regular regimen of sponge baths, acetaminophen, fluids and light clothing over a 24-hour period should drop the fever quite nicely.

SHALL I WAKE THE DOCTOR?

Wake your doctor if you see any of these conditions or combinations:

- Any fever in a baby under two months old
- Any fever that can't be brought down with acetamenophen and sponge baths. Any fever where the child remains uncomfortable and crying after these treatments.
- Any fever over 105°. Chances are good that this is only a virus, but I still want to hear about it.
- Fever with recurrent vomiting
- Fever with severe headache and vomiting
- Fever with severe abdominal pain, which limits the child's ability to walk
- Fever with constant crying. That is crying that won't stop, despite your efforts to distract him.
- Fever with a stiff neck that limits his ability to touch his chin to his chest
- Fever with convulsions

CAN HE GO BACK TO SCHOOL?

The rule of thumb doctors use is that kids can go back to school when the fever has been down for twenty-four hours. We don't impose that rule because of any fear of contagion. Actually, with many viral illnesses, people are contagious a day or two before the symptoms appear. So you needn't keep your child home for fear of exposing other kids in the class. Chances are, that's already been done.

The reason we wait a full twenty-four hours is that some fevers will spike only once a day. That means that your child will run a fever in the afternoon or early evening, but wake up fever-free. Should you send him to school? No. He may be okay, but you're running the risk that later on in the day you are going to get a frantic call from the school nurse asking you to come pick your feverish child up. If you wait a full twenty-four hours from the last fever, that's less likely to happen.

The exception to this rule is chicken pox. With chicken pox, let the rash be the guide, not the fever. That's because the fever generally ends before the contagion does. A child is considered no longer contagious when all the spots are crusted over.

ASK DR. JOHN

QUESTION: We are about to leave on a trip for Europe tomorrow and my four-year-old daughter has just developed a fever of 104°. We can't go without her. Should we cancel the trip?

ANSWER: In the vast majority of ordinarily healthy kids, a fever is simply caused by a virus. If you are going away on an extended vacation out of the country, you might want to drop by your doctor's office before you leave. Statistics are on your side. You might have a kid who is throwing up in your lap on a 747, but the chances are you won't have a child who is seriously ill, or one who is made worse by the trip. The only situation where caution might be advised is if your child has or is susceptible to ear infections. In that case, the pressure changes caused by flying could create a greater risk of rupturing an eardrum.

QUESTION: How contagious is a kid with a fever?

ANSWER: Generally, when you have a fever, you are contagious. But since most fevers are caused by viral illnesses, my feeling is that it is very difficult, if not impossible, to try to keep a kid from exposing her peers at school. Unless there are definite signs of more serious illness, I wouldn't worry too much. I just would presume that every classroom is going to have a certain number of viruses passed around each year, and that's just one of the facts of school life.

QUESTION: Should you really feed a cold and starve a fever?

ANSWER: As far as I know, there's no truth to this old saying.

There aren't any hard and fast rules about what a child with a fever should or shouldn't eat. Sometimes a kid with a fever is more likely to vomit, so until you've figured out the nature of the illness, you might want to go easy on the steak and pizza. And because fevers do cause kids to evaporate more fluids, you want to give the child as much fluid as she will comfortably take. Stick to basic drinks like ginger ale, or diluted apple juice.

QUESTION: My three-year-old is always running a fever. Her six-year-old brother didn't do that. What is her problem?

ANSWER: Kids are different. Two kids with the same virus can run radically different fevers. One can have a temperature that shoots up to 104° and one can run no temperature at all. After a time, parents usually begin to recognize the tendencies in their children and respond accordingly.

CONSTIPATION

At one time or another, nearly everyone gets constipated. Just look at the number of television commercials for products addressing the problem in adults. When it's adults who are constipated, it's uncomfortable and a nuisance. When it's kids who are constipated, it's often a big worry for their parents. There are major underlying worries that don't always get expressed: Is there something seriously wrong with his system? How long is it going to stay wrong? What's going to happen to all that stuff backed up inside there? Are his intestines going to fill up and burst?

Parents often first encounter constipation in their children when the kids are just infants, so their fears are even more acute: How can such a tiny thing hold it in for so long? Why has something gone wrong so soon?

The first thing to remember is that there are two kinds of constipation in children. The first kind is constipation in a child who has never had a normal bowel movement. This kind of constipation is potentially serious. As we will discuss later, it could signal an anatomical abnormality of the intestine that may need to be corrected surgically or medically.

The second kind of constipation is constipation in a baby or child who has usually had normal bowel movements and then experiences a change. This kind of constipation is not usually serious at all. It's not an illness; it's a condition. In fact, it's a condition with a solution.

Persistent, unrelieved constipation should be seen by a doctor, of course, to check if any abnormalities or blockages have developed. But an occasional bout of constipation lasting as long as a week is not at all unusual in young kids. It does require management and care, but it isn't a situation that poses any hazard at all for the child.

What is constipation? Constipation is very hard, hard-to-pass stools. Often, constipation is associated with a long time between bowel movements. But that's not always the case. Some kids go several days between bowel movements, but pass normal stools without any discomfort when they finally do decide to go. Some kids can pass hard stools for several days in a row. Sometimes figuring out the symptoms can be a little bit tricky. A child who hasn't had a bowel movement for several days may simply complain of tummy pain; sometimes he may even have diarrhea. We'll explain why later.

Normally in these chapters we discuss children over six months first, and then talk about the special problems of infants. In this case, however, we're going to reverse that order. The majority of calls I get for constipation are for infants under six months old. Since parents' first experience with constipation in their child will probably occur during the first six months of life, we'll talk about those situations first.

YOUR CHILD UNDER SIX MONTHS

What are a normal newborn's bowel movements like?

There are three phases. The newborn's first bowel movement will be dark green to black, as the baby passes out the substance known as meconium with which he was born. During the middle of the first week of life, he will have transitional bowel movements, which are part meconium and part normal. By the end of the first week, his bowel movements should be normal. Breast-fed babies' normal stools are like mustard in color (yellow) and consistency (semi-liquid). Bottle-fed babies' stools are darker and firmer.

If your newborn has been constipated since birth, has always had hard lumpy stools, has never passed a stool without assistance or has never passed a stool at all, then you need to seek medical attention promptly. You will very quickly know if your baby has this kind of problem, since all normal newborns pass meconium within 24 to 48 hours of birth and begin having normal bowel movements shortly thereafter.

Continuous newborn constipation can signal a number of serious conditions. Some babies are born with a lack of nerve cells in a part of the bowel so that the bowel doesn't push the stool down through the rectum. This condition is called **Hirschsprung's disease**. *Hypothyroidum,* or thyroid deficiency, is associated with early constipation. Luckily, in most states a blood test is done at birth which can detect this condition.

Some babies have a narrowing or malformation of the intestinal tract or anus, meaning that stools get backed up behind the blockage. In some babies, meconium doesn't pass easily, but instead becomes thick and hard to pass. Eventually it plugs up the system, causing an intestinal obstruction. All of these conditions can be corrected with no complications to the baby, but frequently require surgery.

These are all uncommon conditions, and ones that you will be aware of within the first weeks of your baby's life. They all require a doctor's immediate attention.

But what if your infant has been gratifyingly prompt about soiling his diapers on schedule several times a day for several months—and then suddenly goes for two or three days without having a bowel movement? This is a situation that greatly alarms many parents. In fact, it's no real cause for concern.

During the first 12 months of a baby's life, there are two periods when constipation is very common. The first time is in early infancy when the baby is either breast-feeding or being bottle-fed. It is extremely common for a child to go from having several bowel movements a day to having none at all for several days.

What worries parents is the change. Yet in this case, the change itself is nothing to worry about. In fact, it's a healthy sign that the child is growing. The child isn't in fact constipated. He's just changing his bowel habits.

Generally this type of change is self-regulating. This means that as the body goes along, it adjusts to its new abilities and returns to a new, regular schedule. That schedule may not be the same as it was before, but it will be predictable. If in the meantime there are a few days of harder than usual stools, we can usually fix the problem without any medication. Offering the child extra water will probably be enough to loosen up the system and cause him to begin passing softer stools regularly again.

If your baby is formula-fed, you may find that he is passing harder stools. For babies under two months old, we generally just give them additional water. For babies older than two months we find that a little prune juice helps.

Of course, if the new pattern of no bowel movements persists for a long time, you should check with your doctor. Smaller blockages may not have been a problem for the breast-fed baby's more liquid stools, but begin to become a problem when he begins eating solid food. *But generally we know that the child is normal because he has been having normal bowel movements up to that point.*

When solid foods are added, a baby may begin to be constipated for the first time. This can be anywhere between four months and six months of age. Any changes in diet are associated with changes in frequency and consistency of stools. Adding solid foods for the first time is no exception. As the body adjusts to the onslaught of unfamiliar substances, it has to develop new habits. While that is happening, the child may go for several days without a bowel movement; when the bowels do move, they may be hard and passing them may be painful.

There are some foods that are associated with constipation more than others: bananas, rice and cheese are among them. (For this reason bananas and rice, not surprisingly, make up the core of the BRAT diet we use to treat diarrhea; the other two elements are applesauce and toast.) [see: Diarrhea] Eliminating these foods temporarily from the child's diet may help alleviate the problem. Read the section on treatment for suggestions of the kinds of food and drink that can be offered instead to help the child's bowel movement pass more normally.

There may be other symptoms associated with constipation as well. A child who has not had a bowel movement in several days may be fussy and irritable, and show signs of discomfort. But the discomfort should be mild, and the child should otherwise appear well, interested in his toys, easily distracted and alert.

A rare but potentially serious possible problem is **infant botulism.** Infant botulism is rare at least partly because physicians now routinely warn parents against the main cause, which is feeding unpasteurized honey to children under one year of age. Raw honey may contain bacteria which produce a toxin. After 12 months children's systems are able to kill these bacteria; before that, botulism is a potential hazard.

This is a serious condition and requires hospitalization. Constipation is one of the symptoms, but I would stress that it is only one of the symptoms. A child developing infant botulism will also be whiny and lethargic, have a poor appetite and generally seem like a very sick child. So while it's important to be alert, don't confuse the normal whiny discomfort of a constipated kid with the real sickness of a baby with infant botulism—especially if you have been diligent and haven't given him any raw honey.

What possible serious consequences can a long bout with ordinary constipation have for a child? The answer is generally none. The baby's tummy will get bloated and uncomfortable, but it won't explode. The worse case is if the stool gets so hard and impacted that it becomes hard to push out. Then the child will get what we call **overflow diarrhea.** The hard stool packs the intestines but diarrhea flows around the edges.

A child with impacted stools will need some help. Sometimes you might need to seek your doctor's help; sometimes home remedies are enough. Read the section on treatment for suggestions on how to help your child.

YOUR OLDER CHILD

If your older child who has had normal bowels for most of his life suddenly becomes regularly constipated over a long period of time, your doctor will want to examine him to see if some anatomical problem has developed. By a long period of time, I mean an off-and-on pattern of constipation that lasts for months.

In older children constipation is only rarely a sign of disease. In older children there are two major causes of constipation: changes in diet and emotional issues. Both of these causes can be alleviated by careful management.

Emotional issues are among the most common causes of constipation. What kind of emotional issues? The birth of a new baby, the move to a new home, a major vacation—anything that in the child's small world is seen as a major change. The constipation almost always starts with the child voluntarily withholding. After a while it becomes a habit, and constipation results. That in turn causes painful bowel movements, which makes the child even less willing to go.

Kids also can get constipated when they begin **toilet training.** One possible reason is just sheer confusion. After having been able to move his bowels any time he wanted and in any place he wanted, he is suddenly being asked to hold it. Here's a common scenario: You're in the mall when he suddenly announces he has to go. You know the toilets in the mall are none too clean, and you're ready to leave anyway. So you ask him if he can hold it till you get home. It's only a short ride back—less than ten minutes—but by the time he gets home, his urge has passed. He's engrossed in his toys, and he doesn't go. What's more, he's become used to holding it, which he keeps on doing until he gets constipated.

If there is any stress or conflict around toilet training—and very often there is—the child may simply decide to settle the issue by not going at all. A three-year-old who decides he's not going to go can constipate himself really quickly. This can happen especially in families who believe in late toilet training. If the toilet training has been left until your child is over three years old, you may find that you are toilet training him just as he's developmentally entering into his peak time of defiance. Combine defiance and independence with a need to control the bowels and you may get extra control—and constipation.

This is a case where parents need to work out a plan to ease the immediate situation and to work on the underlying conditions that are causing the constipation. Exactly how you do it is more up to you and your family. Trying to reduce the child's stress over the changes in his life may help. Putting him back in diapers for a little while and starting over a few days later may help too. **Remember: Sooner or later, he will be toilet trained.**

Then read the section on Treatment to relieve the immediate constipation.

CHECKLIST

CONSTIPATED FROM BIRTH: Suspect physical abnormality and seek immediate medical attention.

OCCASIONAL CONSTIPATION DEVELOPS BEFORE SIX MONTHS: Consider **dietary changes** and adjust child's diet. Use natural laxatives or suppositories to assist bowel movements.

DIARRHEA (IN A CHILD WHO WAS CONSTIPATED, OR WHO HAS GONE A LONG TIME BETWEEN BOWEL MOVEMENTS): Consider **overflow diarrhea** and treat for constipation.

OCCASIONAL CONSTIPATION DEVELOPS AFTER SIX MONTHS: Consider **dietary changes** or **emotional issues.** Evaluate child's circumstances and treat accordingly.

PERSISTENT CONSTIPATION DEVELOPS AFTER SIX MONTHS: Consider **physical abnormality** and consult physician.

TREATMENT

My rule of thumb in treating constipation in children is "the simpler the better." Start out with the easiest remedies and work up gradually. Our two goals are to ease his current constipation and to make future bowel movements easier and quicker to pass.

One word of warning about enemas: Don't use them. While they may be commonly used in stimulating bowel movements in adults, we rarely use them with children. Not only are they uncomfortable and traumatic for the child, but there is a risk of perforating the child's intestine. Instead, with children we use soft glycerin suppositories to stimulate the bowels to move and to soften up the stool. Even at that, suppositories are about the most extreme remedy I usually prescribe.

To relieve constipation in infants, we first try adding water to his diet to help soften the stools. If that doesn't prove effective, then we turn to a natural laxative. If necessary, your doctor can prescribe such medicine. Many doctors also recommend adding fruit juice to the diet.

In babies older than six months who are eating solid food, we try dietary management. Prune juice in small quantities helps. So does increased fiber in the diet. That means feeding him more cereals, fruits and vegetables. If your child is drinking a quart of milk a day, gnawing on hunks of cheddar cheese and knocking back a banana or two, you may have your explanation for his constipation right there. Try switching to grapes, substituting some juice for the milk, and a bowl of cereal for some of the cheese.

In children over a year of age, we have more leeway in using medication. Just as with younger kids, we start with dietary management and extra water and then move if necessary to glycerin suppositories. With older children though, we can also judiciously use mineral oil, milk of magnesia or a fiber supplement. All of these will help stimulate the bowels, and ease constipation. Check with your doctor before administering these remedies though.

SHALL I WAKE THE DOCTOR?

Most parents realize that there's no need to call a doctor at night or rush to the emergency room for a bout with constipation. The problem is that many parents aren't always sure that it is constipation. That's because the symptom they see is abdominal pain, and a crying child. Many's the time I've been roused from a sound sleep by a frantic parent who only under my drowsy questioning remembers that the child hasn't had a bowel movement for several days.

Of course we are always on the alert for appendicitis. If you suspect appendicitis, by all means consult your doctor immediately. Consult the abdominal pain section in the "Crying and Pain" chapter for more information.

If your child keeps you up late crying and complaining of abdominal pain, ask yourself when the last bowel movement was. If you can't remember or know that it was a long time ago, try stimulating the child's bowels. **Do not give laxatives, mineral oil or milk of magnesia.** Those could prove harmful if your child actually does have appendicitis. Instead, try a glycerin suppository. (Many parents keep them on hand for just such late nights.) Glycerin suppositories should stimulate the bowels to move within ten or fifteen minutes. If they don't work within that time, try another one. If the second dose doesn't work, consult your physician immediately. And of course, if you have any doubts at all, call.

CAN HE GO BACK TO SCHOOL?

The only problem constipation causes that could affect school attendance is a social problem. If the child has been constipated for so long that he is suffering from overflow diarrhea, it could prove embarrassing to him and irksome to the teachers. There aren't any medical reasons why he shouldn't be in school, so consider your own child and discuss things with the school.

ASK DR. JOHN

QUESTION: My doctor suggested using a rectal thermometer to stimulate the bowels. Isn't that dangerous?

ANSWER: Rectal stimulation by thermometer used to be a common recommendation. It stemmed from observations that children often moved their bowels after having their temperatures taken rectally. The stimulation consists of nothing more than inserting the thermometer as if to take the temperature, and then removing it. I have had very good luck with glycerin suppositories which are easy to use, safe and effective. I prefer to recommend that parents keep a small supply around the house.

QUESTION: I've heard that adding corn syrup to the baby's formula helps ease constipation.

ANSWER: I've heard that too. It's one of those old pieces of folk wisdom. I don't know why it would work, but because it is harmless, and enough people tell me it does work, I don't discourage people from trying it.

QUESTION: If my child becomes constipated in the course of toilet training, should I drop the effort?

ANSWER: Don't drop it, just back off for a while. Explain to him that this is something that's got to get done, but that right now you are going to take a break. Then pick it back up in a week or two and try again.

QUESTION: When he finally did pass a stool, it was very difficult and painful. He still seems uncomfortable. What should I do?

ANSWER: Passing a hard stool can cause tiny rips and fissures in the anus that are quite painful. Warm baths help. So does an application of Vaseline or an antibiotic ointment like Bacitracin after each diaper change.

COUGHS

Sometimes I can hear the sound in the background, as the worried parents try to make themselves understood over the noise.

"She's coughing, Doctor," they say. "She's been coughing for hours and I just can't make her stop. What can I do for her?"

And certainly the poor kid sounds miserable. She's hacking away, and sometimes crying in between coughs. A bad cough can be a rough experience for a child, and a frightening one for the parent.

It almost always seems more troubling for the parents because coughing is one of those kids' symptoms that seem to start, or get worse, as soon as you turn out the light for bed. So parents' anxieties about their children's health get compounded by their own worries and indecisions: "Is it really bad enough to call the doctor? At *this* hour? But what if I wait? Then it will be later. How will I feel at 2 a.m. if this still hasn't stopped? Will I have to take her to the emergency room? What if she has pneumonia? What if she coughs so hard she can't breathe? How will the poor little thing sleep coughing like this?" And sometimes, in the midst of all these worries, another more practical and understandable question might creep into a parent's mind: "How am I going to sleep tonight?"

The major reason for parents' turmoil, I believe, is the fear of being out of control, not a fear of any specific disease that the cough might portend. Yes, parents often worry about pneumonia, and it is a reasonable thing to think about when facing a serious cough. But more often, the parents' concerns are about the cough itself. For one thing, the child's discomfort alone can be unsettling. A coughing child is an unhappy child, sometimes crying along with the cough, getting red in the face and sometimes appearing to grow short of breath. As parents, our instincts are to comfort the child, to make it all better. And faced with a bad cough, we sometimes feel ourselves helpless to do enough. For another thing, I often find that parents are worried not just about how serious the cough is now, but about how serious it is going to get if we don't do something about it right away.

And then there is the sheer symbolism of the breath. Any condition that threatens to rob a child of her ability to breathe freely, or perhaps even to cause her to stop breathing altogether, is understandably unsettling to even the most stoic parent.

Nonetheless, I have good news in this area. There are certainly some very serious diseases that are marked by bad coughs. As I shall discuss later, parents of infants under two months old especially should take their babies' coughing very seriously, particularly if it is coupled with a fever. Parents of older children, too, should be alert for the signs I will discuss later on that the cough might be, or turn into, something more serious.

Fortunately, such conditions are rare. Thanks to immunizations, some of the more serious causes of bad coughs are becoming even more rare. What's more, parents don't need to feel helpless or frightened when faced with a bad cough. Coughs—even persistent, difficult, apparently very painful ones—can be very effectively treated by parents. Many of the treatments that I will suggest are simple yet very comforting. They not only work against the cough, but give the opportunity for some good Mommy or Daddy snuggling, which is always good medicine for a sick kid.

WINTER COUGHS

The first thing we need to think about when we evaluate a cough is what time of year it is. Of course, for most parents that's not too taxing. Chances are, if you live in the two-thirds of the country where winter blows cold, you have had plenty of time to get fed up with the weather by the time you get around to calling me. Freezing wind and sleet, slushy streets, snowsuits that won't zip, lost mittens, and lips turned blue from hours outside making forts and throwing snowballs—these are all part of the backdrop for complaints about coughs. I get fifty times as many calls about coughs in the winter as I do in the summer, and the causes for wintertime coughs are naturally different from those I see in the summer. Wintertime coughs are most likely caused by viral infections, and sometimes by bacterial infections. Summertime coughs are most often caused by allergies. Allergic coughs in the summertime frequently have to do with the child's own type of allergy, or the conditions in her own home or vacation spot. Wintertime coughs tend to come in groups. Coughs are so common in the winter that sometimes I can almost guess before I pick up the phone what this next parent's concern is going to be. You, as parents, will probably note this phenomenon too: Not only your child, but your child's best friend will be coughing. The preschool may be missing three kids and one of the teachers may even be out.

THE BREATHING TREE

The next thing the parents and I try to determine is where the cough is located. Most parents tend to think of all coughs as being the same kind of cough, but they aren't. The questions I ask parents over the phone are designed to help me distinguish among different types of coughs. With a little practice, you can too.

It helps if you think about the child's breathing system as a sort of a tree with three major parts. At the top of this imaginary tree, and closest to the top of the child's body, are the sinuses. In the middle section of the tree, coming down through the middle of the body like a tree trunk, are the larynx and trachea. At the bottom, fanning out like big ballooning roots, are the bronchial tubes. Knowing where the cough originates helps us to decide how to treat it, and whether or not it is likely to be, or to develop into, something more serious.

Before we do this, though, we first need to check to make sure the cough isn't being caused by a foreign body lodged in the child's throat. You could suspect it if your child has been totally normal, with no congestion and no fever, yet suddenly has a coughing attack. Most frequently I find that it is young children who have older brothers and sisters who get things lodged in their throats—usually the little pieces of toys that have escaped their parents' notice.

If it is a foreign body, sometimes your child will be able to tell you. You should also consider the circumstances: Did the cough come on suddenly while the child was eating or playing with some small toys? Does the child consciously seem to be trying to get something irritating out of her throat?

If you think that's your child's problem, get in touch with your doctor immediately. Or, if you can't reach him or her, go immediately to the emergency room. **Don't** stick your fingers down her throat to try to remove the object. You may only push it down farther. A foreign body is a potentially life-threatening situation because of the possibility that the windpipe might be blocked off. So treat this situation with care.

Often, however, I get middle-of-the night calls from parents who suspect that their child has swallowed something. In these cases, it's usually parents confronting croup for the first time. It's the sudden onset of a barking, hoarse cough that often makes parents think that only something stuck in the throat could produce that sound. I'll talk about croup later, how you can recognize it, and what to do about it.

The Top of the Tree: The Sinuses

While many, many adults complain of sinus problems, what the sinuses actually are is still a mystery to most people. Basically, they are little pockets in the face. Some of them are right behind the eyes, some are in the cheeks, and some are right in back of the nose. They exist to help filter the air we breathe, and to manufacture the mucus that lubricates the nasal passages. But like anything that exists for a purpose, they can also get sick.

Although the sinuses seem far removed from the site of the cough—which almost always seems to be in the throat—the sinuses are statistically far and away the leading cause of coughing in children. Coughs coming from the upper part of the respiratory system are also far and away the least serious of the three kinds of coughing and don't always require immediate medical attention.

These coughs are less serious because they are actually just a reaction to another condition: the drainage of fluid from the sinuses. When the sinuses get infected or respond to an allergy, they get stirred up to make more mucus than they usually do. They make so much mucus that it becomes trapped inside the sinuses. When the sinus outlets swell, the trapped mucus presses painfully against the face.

But when the excess mucus begins to drain, it drips down the back of the throat. It is that dripping mucus that activates the cough center. The cough center is at a spot in the throat just before the trachea divides into two parts (one on each side) to branch out into the two lungs. When the cough center is activated by dripping mucus, it sends a message to the brain. The body coughs, driving the mucus back up the windpipe where it can be spit out or swallowed. This is a very useful function: It keeps mucus and other foreign bodies out of the lungs where it could do harm. It may be a nuisance, but it's a job that has to be done. You might say that a child's cough to clear mucus from the throat is actually a very healthy response.

How can you tell if a cough is being triggered from draining sinuses? Well, in the first place, you can usually see that your child has a runny nose. This kind of cough is usually associated with the kind of cold that sends mothers and fathers darting across the room with tissues a dozen times a day. Sometimes the child will complain of stuffiness instead. But even though the mucus isn't running out the front of her nose doesn't mean it isn't running out the back and down her throat. One other sign to look for: Sinus-related coughs usually get worse at night, or whenever your child lies down. That's because when she's lying down, her sinuses still drain freely, causing the mucus to pool in the windpipe. When the windpipe clogs, the cough reflex takes over, and the coughing begins.

Such a cough also sounds different. When parents call, they often describe this kind of a cough as a "loose" cough. You can hear your child coughing up phlegm, and sometimes there is a rattle in the throat. That rattle is caused by nothing more than the child's breath vibrating past some "un-coughed-up" phlegm.

These coughs can often go on for a long time, as long as a runny nose can run, actually. That could mean a week to ten days of coughing. Sometimes—especially in school age children, or children with older siblings—one runny nose leads to another, and colds and coughs seem to go on all winter.

I wouldn't be automatically concerned if such a cough dragged on. But after a week to ten days, I would begin to look closely at the child to see if there are other signs that an ordinary draining sinus might have evolved into something else.

If the cough persists, look at the child's overall level of health. Is she starting to seem sicker, more listless, perhaps with bags under her eyes and maybe a little fever day or night? If so, I would suspect that the ordinary cold has developed into a **sinus infection.**

Often I find that a sinus infection has developed in a child who seems to be recovering nicely. The parent will come in and say that the child seemed to be getting better, but then began drooping about and complaining of a headache.

The clearest evidence of a sinus infection is the color and consistency of the mucus. Discharge from the nose and throat of a sick kid with a garden-variety viral infection is clear to dark grayish-green in color and is light to moderately sticky. With a sinus infection, the color and thickness of the discharge changes. It becomes much thicker and sticky. The color changes and can run from a dark green to a very bright yellow.

A potential sinus infection should be looked at by your doctor. While untreated viral infections will sooner or later clear up by themselves, sinus infections are caused by bacteria invading the sinuses. So a sinus infection needs to be treated with antibiotics. Still, the main problem in treating sinus infections is treating the child's discomfort. So check the treatments below.

The Middle: The Throat

The most common cause of a cough coming from this middle section is a viral infection that has irritated the child's larynx (epiglottis) and trachea.

A cough coming from the middle section sounds different from one set off by sinus drainage. This cough is a dry, hacking cough. Sometimes the child will feel and act as if there is something in the throat that can't be cleared or soothed. But it isn't like the wet cough from sinus drainage. This kind of middle-area cough usually doesn't bring up any phlegm.

If parents observe closely enough, often they can notice that certain things will trigger a cough of this kind. When the child first goes outside, for example, the cold air blowing across the irritated trachea may set off a fit of coughing. Rough activity can set it off; you may see a child who is well enough to run around and climb the monkey bars suddenly break into a fit of coughing. In cases of more sensitive irritation, talking, laughing or even deep breathing can set off coughing.

While the cough from a sinus drip gets worse at nighttime, the mid-area cough is often worse in the daytime, and can actually sometimes be relieved by lying down or sleeping. Still, the irritation or tickling can sometimes cause a bout of coughing in the middle of the night. A change in position may help a sinus-related cough; mid-level coughs aren't affected as much by position.

Sometimes, however, these coughs in young children tend to

blend together. That's because a child will sometimes have a virus that has infected her whole upper respiratory system from her sinuses down to her trachea. She will have an irritated cough, and a wet cough at the same time.

Coughs that originate in the middle part of this tree are annoying, and often very uncomfortable for the little ones. But like upper respiratory coughs, they usually aren't serious causes for worry. There are a few things parents should still look for, and check with the doctor if they have any doubts at all.

While it isn't unusual in any of these coughs for the child to run a little fever—especially at night—a child with a fever, persistent cough, and signs of hoarseness or difficulty in speaking needs special attention. Talk to your doctor about this, because such symptoms could be a sign of **croup.** Croup is nothing more than laryngitis in people under five. There are two causes of croup: viruses and bacteria. Viral croup is by far the more common of the two.

In little people, viral croup is caused by the same viruses that infect adults' larynxes and cause them to lose their voice. In children, viral croup gives a child a very distinctive-sounding cough. It's a high, barking cough. I often compare it to the sound of a seal because the brassy, explosive sound is so much like that of a seal begging for its dinner. There is also a noticeable change in the sound of the child's breath as she breathes in after a cough. The harsh, raspy sound of a croupy child's inhalation sounds a lot like the dreadful villain Darth Vader makes behind his grilled mask. The sound is a direct function of the size of the larynx. In an adult, the larynx is bigger than in a child and the air can pass through infected, swollen larynxes without making that raspy sound.

A croupy cough is a very scary sound, and I don't know any doctor who would be upset to get a call at any time from a parent with a croupy kid. Croup can be a serious condition because of the possibility that the swelling might close off air passages. In the vast majority of the cases I see, the croup passes uneventfully if the treatment I suggest is followed at home. Still, I like my patients' parents to keep in touch with me and be prepared to bring the child in to the emergency room if things get much worse.

The first thing I suggest, as I will describe in more detail later, is a good dose of steam in the bathroom. The steam helps relieve the swelling, and should bring an end to the attack in just a few minutes. If that doesn't work, I then suggest that parents bring the child out into the cold air. Cold air often has the same relieving effect on a croupy cough. If the croup does not appear to be abating after ten or fifteen minutes, I would advise a call back to the doctor and preparations for a possible trip to the emergency room.

In any case, if the child can't drink, is drooling and appears to be turning blue, *don't wait.* Get the child help immediately; for these are signs that the airway is becoming obstructed. Watch how the child breathes. If she is using her whole body, heaving her shoulders as if in great effort, get help.

Fortunately, however, these situations are rare. In most cases, the steam should relieve the worst of the coughing in just a few minutes.

With viral croup, the child may run a fever and appear sicker than a child with another type of cough. Usually viral croup will come on gradually, with a milder cough slowly metamorphosing into the harsher, more painful croupy cough.

Bacterial croup is much more serious and, fortunately, much more rare. Where a viral croup will come on gradually, a bacterial croup comes on suddenly. Viral croup will be preceded by a cold for a day or two. A child with bacterial croup on the other hand will go from normal to very sick in a few hours, often with no cold. The child with viral croup will often have had a mild fever for several days. A child with bacterial croup runs a sudden, very high fever, accompanied by shaking and chills.

Bacterial croup is a very serious illness, but fortunately with the development of the Hib vaccine, one of the leading causes of bacterial croup has been removed. The Hib vaccine is commonly given at two months, four months, six months and 15 months, so babies older than four months have protection against this condition.

Viral croup can also be a serious illness, sometimes requiring hospitalization. But usually I find that most parents can treat the symptoms of the croup effectively at home, using methods I will describe later, and can keep the child comfortable until the virus abates on its own.

Lower: The Lungs

The coughs that originate from the lower part of the respiratory system are potentially the most serious and, for parents, potentially the most worrisome. I get many calls from parents in the wintertime who are concerned about that troubling rattle in their little girl's chest. "Is it **pneumonia,** doctor?" they will ask.

Their concern is understandable. Pneumonia can be a very serious illness, particularly for infants under two months of age. A tiny baby can become sick very quickly, and can need immediate medical attention. In years gone by, pneumonia in adults and children was frequently a cause for alarm, because it was often a life-threatening disease.

Without minimizing the need for vigilance, I would like to express several notes of reassurance. For parents of infants: In today's world of antibiotics, even the most serious forms of bacterial pneumonia can be effectively treated. Prompt medical attention can assure that your child will suffer no ill effects of her bout with this illness. For parents of older children: Pneumonia is by and large not a life-threatening condition. In fact, it is often not a very serious condition at all.

What's more, the one symptom that parents most likely associate with pneumonia—that rattling in the chest—is in fact one of the least likely signs of pneumonia. **You can't hear pneumonia.** The rattling you hear is from your child's breath rasping past the mucus in the windpipe. The rattling, which is usually coming from the child's larynx area (higher up near the collar bone), echoes through the chest cavity and sounds like it is coming from the chest. This rattling, therefore, is much more likely to be a sign that your child is suffering from a cough caused by nasal drip, as we discussed earlier in this section.

The sound of pneumonia is more like a whisper. When the little sacks in the lungs called alveoli get infected, the air passing into them makes tiny little crackling sounds like a piece of cellophane being shaken. In medical school, they told us that we could approximate the sound of pneumonia by pulling our hair over our ears and rubbing the strands together. In any case, these sounds are inaudible to the human ear without the aid of a stethoscope. We can't diagnose pneumonia without examining the child.

A lot of times cases of pneumonia in children are mild. Most pneumonia in kids is what we call **walking pneumonia.** It's a pneumonia that doesn't make a child very sick, and doesn't require any special treatment. In fact, I believe many cases of pneumonia go undetected, and often pneumonia is only diagnosed by the physician in the course of looking at other things.

If certain symptoms do suggest pneumonia, however, I will frequently ask for a chest x-ray even if the child isn't very sick. That is because I want to try to distinguish between viral pneumonia and **bacterial pneumonia.** As with many other conditions, the bacterial version of pneumonia is much more serious and requires much closer monitoring and treatment.

With bacterial pneumonia, the symptoms are usually much clearer. An older child will complain of chest pain; she will feel chilled, even when she is covered up. She may be shaking. She can run a high fever, and looks very sick. While children with viral pneumonia are often well enough to play at close to their normal level, a child with bacterial pneumonia doesn't want to get up to do anything. She appears tired and lethargic.

Also check for an increased breathing rate. The child will be breathing more rapidly because she needs to take in more oxygen. Normally, a child will breathe about 20 times a minute. Much more rapid breathing or labored breathing might also lead you to suspect pneumonia.

Because a child with bacterial pneumonia can get very sick very fast, I recommend immediate medical attention if you feel that your child is experiencing these symptoms. Be reassured: Bacterial pneumonia is rare. Over 90% of the pneumonias I see are viral. But it is better to make sure, if you have any doubts. What's more, it is always possible that a case of viral pneumonia will develop into a bacterial infection when the mucus buildup allows bacteria to breed. So close monitoring is essential.

If your child has a persistent, hacking cough while awake, it could be a symptom of **bronchitis.** Bronchitis frequently follows an ordinary cold or flu. That happens when the bronchial tubes become infected. The bronchial tubes are the main tubes that branch off the trachea and provide the passage of air directly into and out of the lungs. When these tubes become infected or irritated, they produce mucus, which in turn triggers the cough.

A child with mild bronchitis will still be well enough to feel like running and playing, and often we see that running and cold air will make the cough worse. Again, unlike upper respiratory coughs, a bronchial cough may actually get better at night.

Bronchitis, like pneumonia, can be caused either by a virus or by bacteria. And again like pneumonia, the bacterial version is more serious. So if you suspect bronchitis, contact your doctor as soon as possible so that your child can be checked. Your pediatrician will check her chest with a stethoscope to listen for the characteristic rattle of bronchitis, as the wind passes through the mucus-lined bronchial tubes. With bronchitis there is sometimes a mild wheeze that you can hear with your ears. But usually the sounds of bronchitis can only be heard through a stethoscope.

A wheezing noise is also characteristic of an altogether different condition. **Asthma** is an increasing problem, and the most common serious illness facing both children and adults in this country. It's the most common illness that requires good ongoing management, and it's one of the leading causes of visits to emergency rooms.

An asthmatic child will be coughing and wheezing, with a characteristic whistling sound when she breathes out. She will seem to have trouble breathing, trouble getting enough air, and will act and feel like she is smothering.

For parents facing a middle-of-the-night cough, however, one word of reassurance: Asthma is a chronic condition. We don't use the diagnosis of asthma unless there have been repeated episodes. The fact that it is a chronic condition means that parents will have to be vigilant, and become familiar with ways of managing the condition.

Still it does have one bright side. Asthma is not a disease that will usually sneak up on you in the middle of the night. By observation and experience and consultations with your doctor over a couple of episodes of wheezing, you will be able to determine that your child is asthmatic, and begin to learn how to best care for your child.

What's more, in many, many cases of asthma that we see, there is already some family history of asthma. A parent, a sibling or some other close relative is already likely to have had some experience with the condition.

Asthma is basically caused by a spasm of the bronchii—the little tubes that branch out into the lungs and lead the air to the alveoli (the little sacs in the lungs). This spasm often follows a cold, or a flu. Or sometimes it is caused by a reaction to animal dander, dust, mold, air pollution or an allergy to some other substance. No one knows precisely why some people react to these substances this way, or even why a child may react on one occasion but not on another. We do know, however, that genetics can play a role in predisposing a child to asthma. We also know that emotional stress can contribute to both the frequency of asthma attacks and to their severity.

I find that children with asthma, if they are old enough to speak and reason clearly, can frequently predict an attack coming on. They will feel some sort of a reaction in their chest, perhaps a funny buzzing sensation, followed by a feeling of tightness. Children and parents who become sensitive to these signals can greatly help reduce the severity of an attack by beginning treatments before it becomes full-blown. There are many very effective and available treatments for asthma that I will discuss in the treatment section below.

One of the best treatments for children prone to asthma is avoidance. Experience will help parents decide if it is colds, dust, wool or animals that trigger their child's asthma. Knowing these trigger factors helps you avoid them. Medication, too, can be helpful. Exercise-induced asthma for example can be controlled by using medication before any planned exhertion.

The good news for parents is that many asthmatic children frequently grow out of this condition.

OTHER CAUSES OF COUGHS

One other potentially serious possible cause of coughs in children under two years old is **RSV—Respiratory Syncytial Virus.** It causes a cough and a wheeze that is kind of like bronchitis in very young children. If your child under two years old is breathing rapidly, having difficulty breathing, and has a lot of severe coughing, call the doctor immediately because this illness can be severe enough to require hospitalization.

Finally, one last, very preventable cause of coughing and sore throats in children: smokers cough. It is now very well documented that children in homes where one or both parents smoke get more severe and more frequent colds and flus than children of nonsmokers. And not only does the secondary smoke from parents' cigarettes lead to an irritated type of cough, the irritation of the smoke makes the child's throat and respiratory system much more vulnerable to other types of infection. You could be causing your child's illness. Stop smoking now.

THE SUMMERTIME COUGH

While summertime colds and flus aren't impossible, coughs in the summer are usually caused by **allergies.** Allergies can cause the same symptoms you'll find when your child has a cold. The big difference is that allergies aren't associated with a fever. Your allergic child can have a red, runny nose, a persistent cough and red eyes. She may also say she is itchy—that her nose itches or her chin itches.

One major way of treating allergies is prevention. If you know your child is allergic to dust, cat dander or pollen, do your best to minimize the exposure to it. In more extreme cases, desensitization may be helpful.

In the meantime, the common remedies I discuss are also effective at relieving some of the child's discomfort.

YOUR CHILD UNDER SIX MONTHS

Any cough in a very young infant is something that your doctor needs to know about. In a child under two months, the risk of **bacterial pneumonia** is increased, and serious. Bacterial pneumonia in an infant can become life-threatening in under 24 hours. So treat your baby's cough more seriously than you do that of her older brothers and sisters.

Always call your doctor. Now this doesn't mean that every cough in a child under two months is *going* to become life-threatening, just that it *might*. Babies, especially those with older siblings, can often get quite serious coughs. But if you see your baby coughing so severely that she can't breathe, or so that it interferes with her feeding, be more concerned. A baby with just a run-of-the-mill cough should perk up and feed nicely between episodes. A very persistent cough, or a cough accompanied by a high fever, or one where the child's lips turn blue should set off alarms in parents. Call the doctor immediately and be prepared to go for more help if necessary.

Another possibility in very young children is whooping cough. Most children are protected against this by vaccine, but in children who aren't, we still do see this disease. You will see a spasm of coughing so severe that the child will lose her breath. The characteristic whoop comes on the inhalation. The baby is so severely out of breath from coughing that she is literally gasping for her next breath.

Because whooping cough rarely comes on suddenly, we hope we can make the diagnosis before the child reaches the whooping stage. The disease can become life-threatening and require hospital treatment. It's a difficult diagnosis to make, so this is my recommendation to parents: If your child is under six months old, call the doctor for any cough.

CHECKLIST

COUGHING THAT COMES ON SUDDENLY, THAT ISN'T ACCOMPANIED BY ANY OTHER SIGNS OF ILLNESS: Check for signs of a swallowed object. Seek immediate medical attention if it appears likely the child has something lodged in her throat.

LOOSE, "WET-SOUNDING" COUGH WITH A RUNNY OR STUFFY NOSE AND POSSIBLY SOME FEVER: Suspect sinus drainage from a cold. Attempt home treatment with steam and possibly with decongestant and watch for further symptoms.

COUGHING THAT HAS PERSISTED FOR SEVERAL DAYS, THAT IS NOW COUPLED WITH A THICK, STICKY, DARK YELLOW OR GREENISH-COLORED NASAL DISCHARGE AND CIRCLES UNDER THE EYES: Suspect a sinus infection and consult your pediatrician, as antibiotics may be necessary.

DRY, HACKING COUGH THAT SEEMS WORSE AFTER EXERTION: Suspect an irritation in the middle portion of the breathing system, usually viral. Attempt home treatment with steam, lollipops or cough drops, or a cough suppressant if necessary.

RAPID BREATHING, DIFFICULTY IN BREATHING, AND SEVERE COUGHING IN CHILDREN UNDER TWO YEARS: Consider RSV (respiratory syncytial virus) and consult physician immediately.

A BARKING, SEAL-LIKE COUGH WITH A HARSH, RASPING INTAKE OF BREATH, OFTEN COMBINED WITH A FEVER: Suspect croup. Attempt home treatment with steam and call the doctor.

A BARKING, SEAL-LIKE COUGH WITH FEVER, AND NOTICEABLE TROUBLE BREATHING. A BLUISH TINGE ABOUT THE MOUTH: Severe croup. Seek immediate medical attention.

A COUGH ACCOMPANIED BY A HIGH FEVER AND CHANGES TO THE CHILD'S APPEARANCE AND BEHAVIOR, LIKE LISTLESSNESS, AND AN INCREASED BREATHING RATE: Suspect pneumonia. Call your doctor.

COUGHING COMBINED WITH A HIGH FEVER, CHEST PAINS, CHILLS AND SHAKING, OFTEN BEGINNING VERY SUDDENLY: Possibly bacterial pneumonia. Seek medical treatment without delay.

A PERSISTENT DRY HACKING COUGH MADE WORSE BY EXERCISE, LAUGHING OR DEEP BREATHING: Possibly bronchitis. Call your doctor.

A WHEEZING COUGH, ACCOMPANIED BY DIFFICULTY BREATHING: Possibly asthma. This requires several episodes before diagnosis. Consult your pediatrician and attempt home treatment with steam.

A COUGH COUPLED WITH COMPLAINTS OF A SORE THROAT: In the summer, suspect allergies. Consult with the physician, who may prescribe antihistamines. In the winter, suspect a viral throat inflammation or strep throat. Treat with steam, hard candies, lollipops, or cough drops, liquids and rest. Call your doctor for a throat culture.

COUGH COUPLED WITH RED OR BURNING EYES, WITHOUT A FEVER, IN A HOME WHERE ONE OR BOTH PARENTS SMOKE: Smokers' cough. This condition will recur as long as the smoking continues.

TREATMENT

The first line of defense in treating a coughing child is to change her position. If the coughing begins at night when she lies down to sleep, sit her back up again. You could try building a little nest of pillows and blankets so that she can go to sleep propped up in a semi-reclining position. You might even try putting her in her infant seat, or her car seat. That way, if the coughing is caused by **sinus drainage,** the pooling of mucus near the cough center is minimized. Sometimes if you have the time or the inclination, I would suggest that you simply snuggle your little one to sleep semi-upright in your arms. That often is effective against two symptoms—the coughing and the general misery that flu causes a kid. Then when she falls asleep you can lie her down in her own bed.

A child with a cough from the middle or lower respiratory tract might, on the other hand, benefit from slowing down. Since activity triggers these kinds of coughs, try to get your little one to settle down for a while. That's not always easy to do when the child is sick enough to be cranky but not sick enough to lie down. I tell parents that that's one appropriate use of videos and TV.

Steam is a marvelous remedy for nearly all kinds of coughs: **colds, croup, sinusitis, bronchitis, bronchiolitis, pneumonia, asthma, allergy,** or coughs caused by **throat irritation.** That's one of the reasons I say that your child's cough is hazardous to your bathroom wallpaper. One of the best ways to administer steam is to hold the child upright on your lap in the bathroom with a hot shower running full blast. If you have a tub, put in the plug to hold the hot water in. Even a very croupy child usually responds to this steam treatment in just five or ten minutes. That's because the steam penetrates down into the breathing tubes, helping to dissolve the thick mucus there and relax the spasms. Steam also helps clear away the sinus passages and reduce the drainage from that area.

Steam is so effective in treating coughs it is almost automatic that I ask parents to try it first. A child who doesn't respond to steam, however, and also has serious breathing difficulties should have prompt medical attention.

I also caution against using any of the medicated preparations that are marketed for use in vaporizers or other steam producers. While the smell of camphor that is the main active ingredient of most of these preparations probably has a nostalgic, healing association for many of us, in fact these medicines can actually irritate the breathing passages and prolong the cough.

Cough medicines are among the most common over-the-counter remedies. I do recommend them for my patients, but I find that most parents aren't clear on what the different medicines do. These days, drug companies have the habit of putting two or three different medicines into one preparation, perhaps on the theory that if you aren't sure what's causing the cough, it's better to cover all the possible causes.

I disagree. I favor giving children as little medicine as possible. Thus, I try to be very specific about the kind of remedy I prescribe.

For cough caused by **sinus drainage,** a **decongestant** is appropriate. A decongestant helps dry up the dripping mucus. Once the drip past the cough center stops, the cough is relieved too.

A **cough suppressant,** like dextromethorphan (DM), is useful for coughs that originate in the middle part of the breathing system. The cough suppressant works directly on the cough center of the brain, causing it to be a little less sensitive to stimulus. This is useful when the child's throat and lower bronchial system have become so irritated that even a very small stimulus—like breathing—triggers coughing. I like to use a cough suppressant in this case because I often see a circular reaction with coughs like this: The cough causes irritation, which causes more coughing, which causes more irritation.

An **antihistamine** helps especially with coughs caused by allergies. Antihistamines are, as the name implies, medications that work on the body's production of histamine. Antihistamines tend to dry up sinus drainage, and are sometimes sold in combination with decongestants. I dislike giving these combinations. Instead, I usually recommend either a decongestant or an antihistamine.

One note: Although cough medicines can be very useful in helping children and their parents to a better night's sleep, I am often loathe to give them out casually.

Because the cough is such a useful, protective device, we don't always want to turn it off artificially with cough-suppressing medicine. The cough may be annoying, but it is doing its job. If we suppress the cough, we might simply be allowing the cough center to relax its vigilance, and setting the stage for more serious problems down the road.

Bronchitis and pneumonia will frequently require treatment with antibiotics to keep a viral infection from spiralling into a more dangerous bacterial one. Typically your doctor might prescribe amoxicillin or erythromycin or a cephalosporin all in children's pleasant-tasting forms. In the meantime, both bronchitis and pneumonia also benefit from the steam treatments described earlier.

Cough drops can be useful in soothing the irritation for older children. With younger children, I would be more careful because of the danger of choking. A younger child might be given a lollipop instead, with nearly as good a result.

Treating asthma is a little more complicated, and of course requires a physician's assistance. Children over four or five can be taught to use an inhaler, which mists a special medicine that reduces swelling and spasm in the bronchial tubes. Some children with severe asthma will use the inhaler preventatively two to four times a day, even when they aren't in the middle of an attack.

Indeed, as with many conditions, prevention is important for asthma sufferers. I counsel my patients to begin their asthma treatments at the outset of a cold, rather than waiting for the asthma attack, or even to begin treatments with the asthma medications I have prescribed as soon as the cold weather starts.

SHALL I WAKE THE DOCTOR?

Wake your doctor for:

❖ Any cough associated with difficulty breathing. If your child seems to be having trouble catching his breath in between coughs, call the doctor. You may see him breathing rapidly in between coughs, or really heaving his shoulders, using his whole body to breathe.

❖ Any cough where there is a question of an object in the

child's throat. The child may clutch his throat, or you may see drooling and choking.

❖ Coughing spasms that end with a whoop at the end, as the child suddenly takes in breath also need immediate attention. While most kids are immunized against whooping cough these days, the vaccine isn't 100% effective. Call the doctor just to be safe.

❖ Coughing associated with major changes in behavior. I'll get ten coughing calls in a row that I decide simply need reassurance and advice. It's the call I get from a parent who adds that the child is not only coughing, but acting abnormally, that gets my attention. If your child really looks and acts sick, whines and cries and can't be distracted, refuses to engage in some play or watch TV, or refuses to eat or drink, call the doctor. A very sick coughing child could have pneumonia.

CAN HE GO BACK TO SCHOOL?

A leading private school in New York sends home a note with children each year: Don't worry about sending your child to school with a cough, unless the child has a fever or is really miserable. I think that is a sensible attitude. At the end of a bout with a cold, people can have post-nasal drip for a week to ten days. Children usually don't blow their noses well, so the mucus drains down the back of their throats, and they cough. If schools tried to keep every kid with a cough at home, half the kids in the class would be out for half of the winter. So if your child doesn't seem to be made miserable by the cough, send him off to school.

The exception is for a child who has a persistent, dry, hacking cough. That could be a sign of bronchitis. You should consult your pediatrician about such a cough. He or she may tell you to keep the child home to rest and relax. Kids suffering from asthma, too, may need quiet time at home to let the medication take hold and ease the child's discomfort. That's another case where your own physician will know best.

ASK DR. JOHN

QUESTION: I can hear my child coughing at night. She doesn't wake up, and I worry that she might choke on the mucus she coughs up. Should I be watching her closely for this at night?

ANSWER: The natural gag reflex will stop a child from choking on the mucus she produces. If your child is sleeping comfortably and not breathing fast, you don't need to worry about choking.

QUESTION: My daughter's cough just doesn't seem to go away. It's better enough in the daytime for me to send her back to school, but she still coughs pretty regularly all day, and even more at night. Shouldn't I worry that it has gone on so long?

ANSWER: Most doctors say if a cough goes on for more than a week, or in an older child more than ten days, and if home remedies haven't worked, then the child should be examined. In a child who is otherwise not very ill, and not running a fever, a cough can go on for quite some time, especially if one cold runs into another one.

CRYING AND PAIN

A child in pain, evokes just about the most helpless feeling there is for a parent.

In the first place, parents just naturally want to *do* something about it—to stop the pain, make it go away, make everything all better. Deeper down, though, there is fear: What does this pain mean? Is it something more than meets the eye? Is my child really sick? Will it get worse? I get calls all the time for pains that in and of themselves are not serious ones. What is behind those calls is the parents' fears that they are missing something and that some dangerous condition lurks right behind that tummy ache.

As we will see later, fear can be useful as a signal that something should be checked. There are conditions that require a doctor's attention, if only to rule out that there isn't something more serious going on. Some kinds of headaches, stiff necks and tummy aches do mean that you should consult your doctor. And, as always, if you are in doubt, call.

Still, there are many ways of evaluating a child's pain that can make a parent feel less helpless and more able to help the child in a sensible way. If parents learn to look at pain the way a doctor does, they will begin to recognize different kinds of pain. They'll learn to distinguish those that might be serious from those that are just part of normal childhood illnesses that pass.

In a very young baby, unexplained crying has the same effect. As we will discuss later, some kinds of crying can be very distressing to parents simply because the crying itself is so grating and seems so endless. Fear of the unknown, and the baby's inability to say what is wrong, can make these bouts of unexplained crying excruciating for parents.

The trick is to look at the circumstances surrounding the pain. Usually pain does not occur in a vacuum, but is accompanied by other symptoms that can be identified even in very tiny babies. We will go over specific types of pain in this chapter. But no matter where the pain occurs—head, tummy, arms, legs, neck, chest— there are some questions to ask yourself:

❖ When did the pain start?
❖ What were the child's circumstances just before the pain began? Had she been playing? Sleeping? Eating? Acting sick at school or at home?
❖ Does she have a fever?
❖ Does she have any cold symptoms?
❖ Is there diarrhea or constipation?
❖ How does her behavior seem, apart from the pain? Lethargic? Listless? Ready to play, or droopy?
❖ Does the pain seem to be constant, or can she easily be distracted from it?

The answers to these questions will help us pinpoint the likely cause of the pain and what can be done about it.

HEADACHE

When kids get headaches, parents think "brain tumor!" It's natural. We're all concerned about our kids, hoping for the best, fearing for the worst. The rise in first-person magazine accounts and television docu-dramas helps keep the idea of life-threatening illnesses constantly in our minds.

As I said earlier, fear is good because it keeps us vigilant. But that fear should also be put in perspective. I get five calls a week from parents who worry that their child's headache means there's a brain tumor. In fact, in my 20 years of practice, only once have I ever diagnosed a brain tumor in a child.

The fact is that in children, unlike in adults, a headache isn't a reliable signal of a brain tumor. With children, you will see other disturbing symptoms first. Usually you will find that the child has difficulty in walking, has slurred speech or double vision. These are things that parents hardly ever think about and hardly ever see in their children. Usually by the time the headache appears, the tumor has already been diagnosed. Every day, though, I deal with headaches from other causes.

When evaluating headaches in children, the important things to think about are the circumstances surrounding the headache and what the other symptoms are.

Does your "headache-y" child also have a fever? A runny nose? Diarrhea or vomiting? One of the more frequent causes of headaches in kids is **viral illness.** Since there are different kinds of viral illnesses—ones that affect the respiratory system and ones that affect the gastrointestinal system—the headache will be accompanied by other different symptoms. Even dizziness can be a side symptom in headaches.

The best remedy for the headache in that case is the same remedy we prescribe for the viral illness itself: Acetaminophen and rest. The headache will fade along with the virus.

One caution: If your child experiences a headache in combination with vomiting, fever and neck pain, consult your doctor right away. Chances are that your child still has nothing more serious than a viral illness. But because that combination of symptoms can also indicate **meningitis,** you should make sure to get medical advice. See the section on stiff necks for more information.

Many parents find it hard to believe that one common cause of headaches in kids is the same as in adults: **tension.**

"What? What kinds of tensions can she have?" they ask. "She's a kid!"

Well, although it may come as a surprise to some parents, it's completely untrue that childhood is the idyllic, worry-free, stress-free existence we fantasize about for them. All kinds of things in their little lives cause them stress, and stress causes headaches too. The only thing we can do to ease the pain is the same thing we do for our own tension headaches: rest and quiet, cool cloths, and acetaminophen. Children should not be given aspirin because of the possibility that the child has a virus.

What's important, though, is to try to identify and reduce the causes of stress. Are there family problems? Does the teacher say she's having problems in school? Are other kids teasing her or bullying her? Are there things in her environment that frighten her? Just as with adults, kids can benefit from reducing the tensions around them and trying to learn to cope with them.

Also, kids will very commonly complain of bad headaches along with a sensitivity to light. They may want to be in a darkened room. Food or food smells may upset them. So might noise. Frequently they may vomit. All this can seem particularly frightening to parents, especially because the child seems in such very real distress. Symptoms like this can indicate that your child, like some adults you know, suffers from **migraine.**

Consider a child who, after appearing normal and happy during the day, comes in looking droopy and listless, complains of a headache and acts cranky. Think about what she's eaten in the last few hours. Some childhood migraine headaches are related to foods.

So, it's important to look for a pattern, especially in kids who have frequent headaches: Does she get headaches when she comes home from birthday parties? After you stop for a milkshake at McDonald's? On Halloween night? If so, I would suspect chocolate, which is often a culprit. My own daughter troubled me for a long time with her frequent, severe headaches. It wasn't until I figured out the birthday party connection that I was able to help her. Once we banned chocolate from her diet—bingo!—her headaches vanished. And we only had to slip up and give her "just one little piece" of Hershey bar or chocolate cake, and she was right back in the same boat as before.

There is often a family history of migraine. They are more common in the spring and fall, making some people believe that there is some allergic component to migraine. Because of this, we suspect that even very young children may suffer from migraine from time to time, but are unable to articulate their distress clearly enough for us to diagnose correctly.

Treatments include bed rest, acetaminophen and, if necessary, more potent pain killers that your doctor will prescribe.

Because migraine is often associated with vomiting, I suggest that you consult your physician if your child has a severe headache. That's to check for the remote possibility that what the child is suffering from is not migraine, but meningitis.

Here are some common causes of headaches in adults that *aren't* usually causes of headaches in children.

Sinuses: In years past, the medical profession assumed kids didn't have sinus problems. That's wrong. They do. It's just that headache isn't usually one of the symptoms. Adults will frequently have headaches behind the eyes. Such headaches are often quite severe and pounding, and result from the pressure built up in the sinuses. With kids, a more frequent symptom of sinus problems is nighttime coughing (as the mucus drains down the back of the throat) and green sticky nasal discharge and circles under their eyes.

Eyestrain: I often get calls from parents saying that they know their child needs glasses because she is getting headaches all the time. Eyestrain is a common cause of headache in adults, but not in children. That's not to say that children don't need glasses. Many, many children need glasses, and often quite young, but headache isn't one of the common ways you find out about that need.

You generally find out your child needs glasses through a routine checkup. Every child between the ages of five and seven years should be seen by an eye doctor for a screening. If there is a family history of nearsightedness or eye disorders, or if you detect problems with her sight, take her in sooner.

NECK PAIN

Neck pain is an extremely common symptom. So is vomiting. So is headache. When all these symptoms occur together, we become concerned. In 99 cases out of 100, that combination of symptoms will be due to nothing more than that same viral illness. But the combination could also signal **meningitis.** So we need to look closely at a child with that complaint.

One clue we look for: the type of neck pain. With meningitis the neck pain is accompanied by stiffness that makes it hard to move the head up and down. The first thing I will do is have the child stand before me and touch her chin to her chest. You can try the same thing. If she can touch her chin to her chest without discomfort, you should take that to be a reassuring sign.

Even though the combination of neck pain, fever and vomiting is unlikely to be serious, we still like to make sure. This is one combination of symptoms that I would urge you to have examined by a doctor promptly, if only for the reassurance that he or she will give you.

On the other hand if the neck is sore to the touch, and puffed up at the sides, the cause could be **swollen lymph glands.** The possible causes of swollen glands are many, the most likely cause is a **viral infection.** But swollen lymph glands do merit a call to the doctor because they could also be a sign of **strep throat.** Since strep throat is bacterial, it needs treatment with an antibiotic.

Another kind of neck pain from viral illness is a muscular pain that makes it uncomfortable for the child to turn her head from side to side. We call that **torticollis** or **wryneck.** It's caused by a muscle pain associated with the virus.

STOMACH ACHE

Stomach ache is a very common symptom in young children. For most parents an unexplained severe stomach pain leads to the question: Is it **appendicitis?** Chances are it's not. But since appendicitis is a very serious, sometimes life-threatening illness, we try to be extra careful.

There are some ways you can recognize if a stomach pain is more or less likely to signal appendicitis. Again (as with all potentially serious conditions), when in doubt, call! But a little knowledge of how appendicitis usually presents itself will help you reassure yourself. In the vast majority of times, a much simpler explanation will do.

Initially, appendicitis can present itself very much like a gastrointestinal virus, with a low-grade fever and vomiting. But with a viral infection, the symptoms will remain diffuse, with a general feeling of stomach pain, vomiting and nausea. With appendicitis, the stomach pains don't usually remain diffuse. Instead, they gradually become more specific. As time goes on, the pain becomes the dominant symptom. It can be a dull stomach ache, or a severe crampy pain. The key question to ask: Is it a growing, building pain? Many gastrointestinal illnesses can cause quite sudden, sharp pains that can distress a child and her parents a great deal. But in gastrointestinal illnesses, the acute pain is fleeting. Between the sharp cramps, the child will feel better. Appendicitis doesn't act that way. Appendicitis doesn't announce itself with a single severe pain that goes away. Instead, the pain continues, and usually gets worse.

With appendicitis, the pain usually localizes as time goes on. Where does it localize? Draw a horizontal line between your child's belly button and her right side. At the midpoint, a point two or three inches to the right of the belly button, push on the spot. If the child doesn't jump or protest or squeak with pain, we don't usually get too excited right away. Pain in that specific area is one of the sure clues to appendicitis.

Here is a typical phone call I get from a parent:

"Doctor, she's just vomited, and now she's lying on her bed doubled over in pain. She's crying and hugging her stomach. I'm afraid it's appendicitis."

What do we do? We wait. The first thing I will do is ask the parents to watch the child and call back in one or two hours. Nine times out of ten, the parents will call back and say that, while the child is still uncomfortable, the acute pain has passed. That's gastroenteritis. If, on the other hand, the parents call back and say that the child is still doubled over, and is now complaining of a severe pain on the right side, I'll meet that child in the emergency room.

Most parents are frightened of appendixes. They see appendicitis as something abrupt and frightening that will come on without warning and suddenly put their child in danger. It is true that appendicitis can become life-threatening rather quickly. But "rather quickly" is a relative term. While it isn't unusual for a crisis to build and surgery to be performed within six to eight hours of the initial pain, that time period shouldn't cause problems for most parents. If you and your family are going to be manning a remote weather station north of the Arctic Circle, or doing anthropological research in Tanzania, appendicitis can be a serious problem. Or if you routinely go on remote camping trips miles from the nearest paved road, then appendicitis could present a crisis.

In most urban, suburban and even rural areas, however, we usually have some time to watch and make a diagnosis, since appendicitis is a condition that builds over time. If the child lives reasonably close to good medical care—say, less than two hours from a hospital—we have time to watch the symptoms develop.

Usually I try to set parents' minds at ease about their child's conditions. That's often hard to do in the case of appendicitis. Unfortunately, appendicitis pain can mimic almost any kind of abdominal pain. There are whole books written on the subject of diagnosing appendicitis. The best I can do is offer some guidelines. The first is: Don't panic. Appendicitis doesn't usually escalate rapidly into an emergency. The second is that appendicitis is usually a constant, building pain; it keeps on going. Most other kinds of stomach pains go away, but not appendicitis pain. Two hours later, it's worse than it was. Even if it goes away briefly, it comes back stronger—to a point where walking and jumping hurts.

As I said before, most of the time you won't be facing appendicitis, but rather some other kind of stomach pain. What does that leave us with?

The most common cause of stomach pain is a **viral infection.** The child might have sharp crampy pains, a dull, nauseated feeling or just a general feeling of discomfort. Viral infections can hurt almost anywhere throughout the intestinal tract. They can give kids pains in the stomach area, or lower in the intestinal area. Often you will find that the stomach pain is accompanied by cold symptoms, poor appetite, fever, vomiting or diarrhea. Read the "Vomiting," "Diarrhea" and "Fever" chapters for more information on each of those symptoms.

Sometimes, however, that kind of stomach pain will recur. Your child will seem to have viral gastroenteritis over and over again. If this happens, try to pay attention to when it happens and what the child has just eaten. The same type of cramps, nausea or general stomach discomfort may be a sign of **food allergy** or **food intolerance.** It's only after trial and error and a long period of observation that parents often figure out what the offending food is. Once that food (or foods) is removed from the child's diet, the problem goes away.

Another food-related cause of abdominal pain is **gas.** Gas pains usually resolve themselves fairly quickly with the expulsion of gas. But while they are going on, gas pains can be quite acute, crampy and painful.

What about pain in the lower back? An adult might not think of that as stomach pain, but a child who is less able to give a specific description of where it hurts may call this "tummy" pain as well. If your child has a stomach pain, and an ache in the lower back, or at the bottom of the belly over the pubic bone, as well as a fever, you should seek medical attention. With this kind of pain, you might consider a **urinary tract infection.** In this case, however, you will also find not only the stomach pain, but a fever and possible pain or burning on urination. In other words, the stomach pain won't be the only symptom. If you suspect kidney infection—with a fever of 104° to 105°—seek immediate medical attention. Kidney infections can be serious and even life-threatening in extreme cases.

One other kind of stomach pain may come from **constipa-**

tion. We have a whole chapter devoted to constipation, so turn there if you think that might be the problem your child is suffering. It's my experience these days that with both parents working, often they aren't up on their child's bowel habits. So you may not automatically think of constipation because you just haven't noticed that the child hasn't gone to the bathroom in several days. (It helps if day-care centers and caregivers give a daily report.)

The pain of constipation could be vague, with a general feeling of a bloated belly. It can give kids cramps. Sometimes kids lose their appetite and just plain don't feel well, with a generalized dull discomfort. The key to figuring out constipation is figuring out the child's history of bowel movements. If there haven't been any in three to four days, it's more likely that that's the problem.

One warning: If you suspect that constipation is troubling your child, please be careful. If you have any suspicion that it might be caused by something else, call your doctor before you administer any laxatives. If the stomach pain isn't caused by constipation, but rather by appendicitis, laxatives can worsen the situation.

The final kind of stomach ache is one of the more common kinds and also one of the trickiest. It's the stomach pain that doesn't really seem to come from anywhere. Here's a typical call I will get, usually on a Sunday night or early Monday:

> "She seemed fine all weekend. In fact, we were sledding most of the weekend. But on Sunday night she suddenly started saying her stomach hurt. She curled up on her bed and whimpered for a bit Sunday evening, went to sleep, but woke up in the morning saying her stomach still hurt. She didn't have a fever, and wasn't vomiting, but she seemed so uncomfortable that we decided to keep her out of school for the day. By noon she seemed fine. Did she get a 24-hour virus over the weekend? Or did she eat too much or get over-tired?"

What do we do with a complaint like that?

If it happens once or twice, the answer is nothing much. Maybe she did get a little virus. Maybe she was over-tired. If it goes away, and she feels better, then there's nothing to treat, and nothing to worry about. But if a child begins repeated complaining about a stomach ache—one that is elusive, has no other associated symptoms and seems to come and go at will—we need to look for other causes.

Chronic complaints of stomach pain like this may require a trip to the doctor. We need to rule out inflamed appendixes or food allergies. We feel the abdomen to rule out a blockage. We take urine cultures to rule out kidney infections. We take the temperature to see if an elusive fever might have escaped us.

In my experience, 99% of the time the cause of such elusive tummy pain is in the child's life, not in her tummy. In the above case, it's pretty clear that this child has developed a case of **school phobia.** You need to check pretty carefully to see what the reasons might be. Did she lose the library book she was supposed to return Monday morning? Is some other child pestering her at school? Is she having conflicts with her teacher?

While the official term for this is **malingering,** it's important not to let the negative connotations make you unduly abrupt with the child, or to dismiss the symptoms as "faking." While the pain probably has no organic cause, it is nonetheless serving a useful function: It is alerting us to a problem in the child's life that needs addressing. To simply send the child back to school with an admonition would be doing her a disservice. While it isn't a medical problem, the pain in this case is a real symptom of a real problem.

LEG AND ARM PAINS

Here's a scene that almost all parents face from time to time: Your five-year-old goes to bed normally. But two or three hours later, maybe just about the time you are ready to go to bed yourself, she wakes up sobbing. She cries and cries. This child is in real pain. She will grab at her legs, rubbing them and howling, sometimes for quite some time.

Heartbreaking? Very. But also very, very common. We call them **growing pains.** They're a peculiar phenomenon, and not very well understood. All we know is that between five and ten years old in particular, many children suffer from these pains. They often occur during sleep, but they can happen any time—while resting, watching TV or after exercise. They aren't serious pains, and don't signify anything abnormal.

There's no special medical treatment for growing pains, beyond trying to make the child as comfortable as possible. What helps? Massaging the sore spot helps. So does a big dose of TLC from a parent. If the pain persists, you might try hot baths, heating pads or, in extreme cases, acetaminophen. Cramps and sore muscles can give similar kinds of pains.

These kinds of pains are often worrisome to parents who fear that they might signal **bone cancer.** It is true that bone pain can be a symptom of bone cancer, which is far more rare in children than growing pains. But the pain is quite different in cancer. Growing pains are general. They occur all over the bone, on both sides of it, and they come and go. You won't be able to identify one specific place that is painful.

For parents who are really worried, I suggest that they record the location of the pain. If the pain is in different places every time the child complains, I am less concerned. It could be growing pains or stress. If the pain is in the same place every time she mentions it—even if the pain comes and goes—then I would like to see that child.

That's because the pain of cancer occurs in one specific spot. The child will wince or cry out if you press on that spot. It is the kind of pain that might also cause you to think of a **fracture.** In fact, if a child suddenly begins complaining about a specific spot that hurts, fracture is the first thing I would think of. Has she been climbing trees? Did she fall? Slide into third base? Did one of her little friends kick her?

In any case, with a specific bone pain, as opposed to the general discomfort of growing pains, I would suggest a call to your doctor who may in turn suggest an x-ray.

JOINT PAINS

Sometimes children will complain of pain, not in their bones, but in their joints. They won't say joints, of course. But they will be pretty clear about where the pain is. "My elbow." "My knee." "My hands." Joint pains can be as limited as simple discomfort, or severe enough to limit the use of that joint. Sometimes a child's knee will hurt so much, for example, that she will refuse to walk.

The first thing parents think about when their child comes to them complaining that their joints hurt is **arthritis.** Joint pain by itself isn't enough for doctors to consider arthritis as their first diagnosis. A true arthritis involves not only pain, but swelling in the joint.

Juvenile **rheumatoid arthritis** is a real disease. But diagnosing it is tricky, and it isn't a diagnosis we make quickly. Typically we would see a child who complained of joint pain. The pain would sometimes flare up and sometimes settle down. She would complain that her knee or her ankle hurt—usually one of the bigger joints—and perhaps refuse to run or jump. Sometimes the joint would really flare up, and become so inflamed that it would be acutely painful. But more often it would be a long pattern of more subtle pain. Sometimes there might be a fever that comes and goes, but more commonly not.

There are blood tests that help us identify rheumatoid arthritis, but the blood tests often aren't conclusive in children. Usually this is a diagnosis that is made over a long period of time, with much observation.

There are other much more common reasons for joint pain. The most common would be a **viral illness.** She will have symptoms of a cold or a stomach upset and low-grade fever along with the joint pains. The joint pains can be severe enough to cause the child serious discomfort, and even make her want to limit her activity. This usually gets better in a day or two.

Lyme disease is another common cause of joint pain. But you will almost never have joint pain by itself in Lyme disease.

Rather, the joint pain will develop at the end of the illness, which begins with a rash and a fever after a tick bite. In children, the acute phase of Lyme disease is pretty noticeable, including the characteristic bull's-eye rash. Read the chapter on rashes for more information about Lyme disease.

If a child complains of pain in one specific joint, say a single knee, or a single elbow, I would consider **trauma** as a cause. Just as with bone pain, a blow, a fall, a kick or a twist can all cause serious joint pains. Did she fall off her bicycle? Twist her ankle playing soccer?

The treatment for trauma is to put the joint or bone at rest. You don't usually need to immobilize the limb (unless it's broken of course). But you do need to keep the child from bending it, putting too much pressure on it or using it excessively. Often an elastic bandage and a day or so of videos will do the trick.

The difficult part comes when the child wants to resume her normal activities, but finds that these activities cause pain. Here's one common situation parents face: A child twists her ankle on the weekend playing soccer. She wraps it in an elastic bandage, and keeps off it for a day or two. Walking around on it is fine, but then, come Thursday, she goes to ballet class and the ankle hurts a lot again. What should she do? The answer is: Keep away from ballet for a couple of weeks. It's hard for kids to take being told to stay away from their favorite activities, but it's really the only solution. If the joint is still painful, putting stress on it could cause more serious problems down the road, including the possibility of permanent damage.

There's one kind of joint trauma, however, that is particularly common and particularly scary—but surprisingly easy to fix.

Here's the scene: Mommy and Daddy are going for a walk with their child, and playing "Whee!" You know the game, where each parent takes an arm and yells, "One, two, three, whee!" and swings the child up in the air. Everyone is laughing and having a good time until suddenly the child cries out in pain.

Suddenly the child drops her arm to her side where it hangs limp. She cries and whimpers. No amount of persuading will get her to bend her arm.

This panics parents. Their first thought is that they've broken their child's arm. They are frightened and traumatized, not the least because they think it is their fault. Chances are, however, that the problem is much less serious than it appears. Chances are, she has a case of **nursemaid's elbow.**

Nursemaid's elbow is extremely common between the ages of two and five. The tendons are a little more lax at that age, and the joint is a little weaker. A two-year-old doesn't have the muscles that a six-year-old does. (Anyone, of course, can dislocate a joint. It's just that it takes more effort later on.)

Why is it called nursemaid's elbow? This condition got it's name from the way it's caused; it was named after the care-givers of old. Because a child's joint pops out of place so easily, it will pop out at the tug of a nursemaid's hand as she is trying to get her young charges to leave the playground on time, or to stay back when they are approaching a busy street. Parents are often ashamed to admit what happened, because of the stigma associated with hurting their own child. Babysitters can be even more traumatized, and not willing to admit that anything happened.

Despite parents' and babysitters' fears, this condition is very common. I did it myself to my own son once. When we were playing "whee!" crossing the street I felt the elbow pop. Luckily I know what to do. I popped his arm back in so quickly that my wife, who was hanging on to his other arm, didn't even know what had happened.

Nursemaid's elbow looks scary because the child holds his arm at his side and refuses to use it. But as my experience shows it is in fact very easy to fix. I've talked parents through it over the telephone. You may need to consult your doctor if your attempts don't work. Don't force it! But it's worth at least a try before heading to the doctor's office or the emergency room. In fact, I've seen a number of cases where a parent, believing that the child's arm or wrist is broken, have taken her in for an x-ray, only to have the x-ray technician, in the course of moving the arm for the picture, pop the elbow back into place.

One caution: If you have any suspicion that the arm might be broken or fractured, *don't try this.* Nursemaid's elbow is never caused by a fall or a strike. It's always caused by a tug or a jerk of the arm. Be sure you know how the condition arose before you try to fix it.

To start, you hold the child's wrist in one of your hands, and with the other hand, hold the child's arm above the elbow. While stabilizing the upper arm with your hand, turn the wrist gently so that the palm faces the ceiling. At the same time gently flex the arm at the elbow in towards the body. The whole motion should be done smoothly, turning the arm in and up with one slow motion. If it's done correctly the elbow should just pop back into place, and the child should be not much the worse for wear.

If that doesn't work, let your doctor do the job. In either case, once the arm is popped back in, the child should experience only minimal discomfort.

If the arm is popped back into place instantly, there should be no ill effects. If it has been out of place for a while, there may be some lingering discomfort that can be easily relieved by hot baths, hot compresses and acetaminophen.

CHEST PAINS

The first thing to realize is that chest pains usually don't mean the same thing in children that they do in adults.

In a 55-year-old, the first thing we think about when we hear of chest pain is heart attack. That's not so for kids because heart attacks in young children are rare. Chest pains in young children are usually far more benign.

There is one type of chest pain that could indicate a heart condition. If your child suffers from persistent chest pains (that is, pain that doesn't go away in a couple of days) and seems lethargic, with poor appetite and a general appearance of ill health, then consult your doctor. It could be a sign of **myocarditis.** Myocarditis is a viral infection of the heart that causes chest pains. It's more common in older children and adolescents than in younger children. In any case, it isn't common at all.

The most common cause of chest pain in young children is

pulled muscles. Often you'll find these pains along with viral illnesses. That's because children will sometimes cough so hard or vomit so hard that they will pull muscles in their chests. This kind of pain will last for a day or two and then go away on its own.

EAR PAIN

It's many an earache that has kept a worried parent up well into the night. Earaches can be quite painful to children, and until diagnosed can be a frequent cause of unexplained crying and discomfort.

Earaches usually result from **middle ear infections,** from **swimmer's ear,** which is an infection of the external ear canal, or from some **foreign body** lodged in the ear.

Ear infections are usually accompanied by other symptoms of a cold like a runny nose, stuffiness, fever or coughing. These other symptoms could give you a clue that an ear infection might be developing, but that isn't always the case. Ear infections are sometimes the cause for otherwise unexplainable crying. So if your child is crying inconsolably and you can't find any reason for it, consult with your doctor. It may be worth a trip to his or her office just to see if there is some simple way of easing the child's discomfort.

Usually, though, ear pain comes accompanied with other signs that will help you decide where the problem might lie. Suspect an ear infection if your child is crying, tugging at her ear and has a fever. Other typical signs are poor sleeping, fussiness, decreased appetite and diarrhea.

If your child has recently been swimming and complains of ear pain, you might consider swimmer's ear, which is a bacterial infection of the outer ear canal.

Pain in the ear that seems otherwise unexplainable might be explained by some foreign body. Although smaller children who can't talk can't give any clues to their condition, older children may be able to tell you—sometimes with much coaxing—that they've pushed a Lego piece in their ear just to see what would happen.

All three of these conditions require a doctor's care. Inner ear infections and swimmer's ear are both infections that require antibiotic treatment. Objects in the ear require a doctor's attention too, since a parent's attempts to remove the object may simply push it in deeper.

These conditions can, however, wait for the morning and office hours for consultation. In the meantime, read the chapter on ears for suggestions on how to make your child more comfortable.

SORE THROAT

In the summer, one of the most common causes of sore throat is allergies. The substance the child is allergic to, called an allergen, irritates the throat, causing redness and discomfort. Usually the cause is airborne, like pollen or dust. Consult with the physician, who may prescribe antihistamines.

In the winter, the most common cause of sore throat is a **viral illness.** The child's throat will be inflamed and red and he will often exhibit other cold symptoms like a cough, runny nose and stuffiness.

A very young child who can't talk will often indicate a sore throat by trying to jam his fist down his throat, presumably in an effort to get to the place that hurts. Generally these inflammations go away by themselves. The discomfort can be treated with a combination of acetaminophen and hard candies, cough drops or lollipops.

If the sore throat is combined with a fever, however, you should consult your doctor. Sore throats are usually just viral infections, but a child with a sore throat and fever may have **strep throat** which is a bacterial infection that can, if left untreated, lead to a more serious condition,—rheumatic fever—which can damage the heart muscle. If you suspect from observing your child's behavior that he might have a sore throat along with a fever, check with your doctor. He or she may recommend an office visit for a culture.

It used to be that children who got sore throats repeatedly were sent off to have their tonsils removed. That was in the days before good antibiotics were readily available. Today we sometimes still remove tonsils, but usually only if they are abscessed. That means one of childhood's leading causes of hospitalization (and of ice cream consumption) has largely become a memory.

Finally, one last, very preventable cause of coughing and sore throats in children: **smokers' cough.** It is now very well documented that children in homes where one or both parents smoke get more severe and more frequent colds and flus than children of nonsmokers. And not only does the secondary smoke from parents' cigarettes lead to an irritated type of cough, the irritation of the smoke makes the child's throat and respiratory system much more vulnerable to other types of infection. You could be causing your child's illness. Stop smoking now.

EYE PAIN

The most important distinction to make in evaluating eye pain is to decide whether the pain is caused by **disease** or **injury.** In the developed world, diseases of the eye are fairly benign. They can make a child very uncomfortable, but they won't cause permanent damage. Eye injury, however, can be quite serious.

Usually if the pain is accompanied by a redness in both eyes the cause is disease. It is very rare that the kind of trauma that would cause eye injury—a baseball, a little brother, a stick—would affect both eyes at once.

The first thing to do? Ask. An older child can tell you if anything happened. And in many cases there will have been some witness to the younger child's injury such as a sibling, a babysitter or a friend at the park. There is one clear, nonverbal sign in a child of any age: refusal to take the hand away from the eye. Often if there is dust or dirt in the eye, the child will come to you crying and rubbing her eye. If the scratching is not too intense, however, you will be able to persuade her to remove her hand so you can get a look at her eye. If she has been seriously injured, however, no amount of coaxing is going to get that hand away from her eye.

If you suspect injury, seek immediate medical attention. That doesn't mean you should rush to the emergency room every time she gets dirt in her eye. Read the "Eye" chapter, and try to help her. If the dirt or dust is flushed out and an hour or two later she seems to have forgotten the incident and is playing happily, then you can safely assume that the particle has done no harm. But if she continues to complain of a scratchy feeling in her eye, or continues to rub it, then I would suggest you consult a doctor to see if there is a scratch on the cornea also known as **corneal abrasion.** Because of the possibility of infection, even a slight scratch should be observed.

When your child has **eye pain with cold symptoms** like a runny nose, or congestion or a cough, especially at night, this may be **sinusitis.** The sinuses are located right behind the eyes so when they become infected, they put pressure on the eyes, causing pain. A sinus infection should be seen by a doctor who may prescribe antibiotics. In the meantime, you can also use acetaminophen or a decongestant to relieve the pain.

Sometimes other illnesses will first be apparent through a pain in the eyes. A child coming down with **infectious mononucleosis** may first complain of painful eyes, as will a child in the early stages of **flu.** Your course in this case is to check for other symptoms and if you find none, wait and check again.

RECTAL PAIN

Unlike in adults, rectal pain is *not* a sign of rectal cancer.

Instead, the most common cause of rectal pain in children is **constipation.** When the child passes a hard, lumpy stool, it irritates the tissues and causes pain and burning. Read the chapter on constipation if you think this is the source of your child's rectal pain.

Another possible cause is irritation from **diarrhea.** The passage of frequent acidic stools can also inflame the tissues of the rectum. Read the chapter on diarrhea if you think this is the problem.

Kids who are infected with **pinworms** or other parasites may show signs of rectal discomfort or itching. They may also have some rectal bleeding. If you suspect this condition in your child, consult your physician, as this can be treated with medications.

There aren't any other usual medical causes for rectal pain in kids, although rectal pain may be a tip-off to possible sexual abuse. Sexual abuse will usually be accompanied by behavioral changes in children which may include difficulty sleeping, reversion to bed-wetting in a child who has been previously dry, fear of certain people and certain places, and depression.

If you suspect sexual abuse, consult your physician. There are sophisticated teams of doctors, psychologists and social workers at most hospitals who can look into this possibility. By law, such suspicions must be reported.

PAIN ON URINATION

If your child complains that it "hurts when I make wee wee!" or cries, or makes gestures to complain that her genitals itch or burn, she possibly has an **irritated urethra.** Both boys and girls suffer from this condition. It is easier to diagnose in boys than in girls because you will be able to see the redness at the end of the penis. With an irritated urethra, the child will be very uncomfortable, but there won't be any actual infection. You should consult your doctor, but chances are the treatment will consist of a cortisone cream to reduce the irritation, or soothing (non-soapy) baths.

If the pain, irritation, or increased urinary frequency is accompanied by fever, consult your doctor. That's because of the increased likelihood that she has a **urinary tract infection.** Such infections are caused when bacteria travel up the urinary tract from the urethra (the urinary tract opening to the outside of the body). Adults often call the condition a **bladder infection,** but the fact is that any part of the urinary tract can become infected with bacteria.

We diagnose urinary tract infections by doing a urine culture. The treatment consists of antibiotics that are particularly effective against infections in the urinary tract.

If, however, the child complains of pain on urination or even just a "tummy ache," has a high fever (one that spikes as high as 105° or 106° and can't be brought down), looks lethargic and acts listless, take immediate action. This high, spiking fever can mean a serious **kidney infection.** Such a high fever combined with complaints of urinary difficulties or lower back or "tummy" pain should send you right to your doctor or to the emergency room. Kidney infections aren't common, but they aren't rare either. They can also be hazardous, much more dangerous than bladder infections which can sometimes be viral and mild. Kidney infections can lead to blood infections and a very, very sick kid.

As with rectal pain, pain on urination may also be a tip-off to possible sexual abuse.

PAIN IN THE MOUTH

There are three possible causes for mouth pain: one is **allergy or illness;** the second is **accident or injury;** the third is **dental.** Usually the circumstances surrounding the pain will give you the clues you need.

Most cuts involve the inner mouth. Your child will run in screaming with blood dripping from her mouth. She has fallen from her tree house and chomped on the inside of her mouth with her teeth. Such cuts only need to be seen by a doctor if the bleeding doesn't stop in a reasonable amount of time. Even so, the doctor will usually only apply pressure, not sutures, to control the bleeding. Cuts in the inner mouth, usually heal quickly by themselves without suturing and without scarring.

If the cut is on the tongue, however, it is more likely that you will want to consult the doctor. If the cut seems minor, the bleeding stops quickly and the child's discomfort seems minor, you can be safe in letting her return to play. But cuts in the tongue do occasionally require suturing because they tend to bleed more than other cuts, and because they are often deeper than cuts in the cheek. So if the bleeding continues past a few minutes, check with your doctor.

The most common cause for mouth sores is **viruses.** They can occur almost anywhere. Viruses on the corner of the mouth are usually caused by the common herpes simplex virus. These are the kind of reddish painful sores that are usually called cold sores. You can also get them on the gums, or on the chin.

The herpes virus usually causes a single or a few sores at a time, but there are other viruses that cause sores all over the inside of the mouth. Just like with other rashes, viruses can cause spots and rashes all over the inside of the mouth. But calling it a herpes virus shouldn't cause you too much concern. It's just a type of virus. There are lots of other types, like the Coxsackie virus. Some are known by name, and others aren't.

The best treatment is simple pain relief—acetaminophen—until the sores subside.

If the gums become inflamed, you should consider **gingivitis,** a bacterial infection caused by poor dental hygiene. It may have started as a viral infection, but when it gets worse, the gums become inflamed and sore. You should consult with your doctor or dentist on the treatment of gingivitis, which may need to be treated with antibiotics. In the meantime, acetaminophen provides effective relief.

Allergies can cause redness and sores in and around the mouth. With allergies, you will begin to discern a pattern. Does her mouth redden and appear chapped and sore every time she eats tomatoes? Does she get sores around her lips when she eats oranges or drinks orange juice? When she eats walnuts, does she complain of a burning sensation around the mouth?

Teething will also cause mouth pain right up until the child gets her complete set of baby teeth, which may not be until age 15 to 18 months. But because teething commonly starts much earlier, we have chosen to discuss it in the "Your Child Under Six Months" section following.

A whole range of other dental problems can also cause mouth pain. These conditions are beyond the scope of this book, so you will need to consult your dentist.

NIGHTMARES AND NIGHT TERRORS

Nightmares and **night terrors,** which frequently affect children under the age of ten, can cause your child to scream uncontrollably in the middle of the night. This is a frightening experience because parents often think the child is in pain. In the case of nightmares, the child can usually be quickly comforted by the parents. Night terrors, however, may cause the child to scream for as long as a half an hour, no matter what the parent does.

For parents worried that there really is something else seriously wrong, I suggest that they take the child outside. Something about the change of location is often enough to stop the crying. I don't know why, but it seems to work.

YOUR CHILD UNDER SIX MONTHS

In young babies, pain means crying. They have no other way to express their needs. So it's fairly upsetting for parents of a new baby when their child cries for a while. It makes the parents think the child is in pain, severe pain. The idea of their child being in pain, combined with the fear of not knowing for certain what's bothering her, makes parents themselves fairly uncomfortable.

The problem is that in young babies, crying doesn't necessarily mean pain. Very little babies cry a whole lot anyway. When parents come to me with their new babies for their one or two week post-delivery visit, I try to prepare them for the inevitable crying spells. The trick is to try to distinguish ordinary crying from painful crying. It isn't always easy and most parents usually err on the side of caution: They tend to assume their child is in pain.

The first thing to ask yourself is this: How easy is it to distract her from her crying? Does she stop when she is picked up? Does she stop when she is fed? Changed? Taken out of her crib? Given a toy that drifted out of her grasp? Put in her snuggly? Babies instinctively use crying to communicate. So even repeated lusty crying isn't necessarily a problem if you can figure out the solution. Sometimes, of course that solution isn't always a pleasant one. Some babies get in the habit of crying every time they are put down. Or they get to realize that they don't have to stay in the crib if they don't want to. (If they cry long and hard enough, they will be liberated.) This will be your first encounter with one of the unpleasant truths of parenthood: What they want and what you want are going to clash a whole lot.

There are many good books and parents' guides about childhood behavioral issues. All parents have to learn how to handle situations like these and for purposes of pediatrics, you have already learned something important: This is not a disease.

But what of the crying that goes on and on? Crying that continues whether you pick her up, or put her down? Whether you put her in her jumper chair, or a warm bath? Whether you give her a bottle of milk, or juice, or try to nurse her? That is the kind of crying that sends us looking for medical causes.

One note of warning: The quality of the cry means nothing. Kids can shriek like banshees over nothing, and barely whimper for more serious things. I've seen kids in my office go hysterical when their parents put a hat on them. I would have sworn the kid was deranged. On the other hand, I've seen kids panting with pneumonia making only the most pitiful, timid cries. Over the years I've developed a kind of rough rule of thumb. Like all pieces of folk wisdom, it has its limitations, since there are always exceptions. But in general I've found that if a kid is screaming hard, she's probably in reasonable shape. If the problem is something serious like pneumonia or meningitis, after a while the child wears down and gets listless. The listlessness itself is one of the symptoms. A lusty, screaming child may have gas or she may just be hopping mad. She isn't necessarily very sick.

The one exception to that "quality-of-cry" rule of thumb: injury. I've found that most parents sitting in their living room listening to the babbling of their children playing in the next room can easily distinguish the "Alex just took my binky" cry from the "Anna just hit me on the head with the pull-duck" cry. I don't know how to describe it in this book. All I can say is, when you hear it, you will know.

When your child won't stop crying, you need to begin asking yourself some other questions. Your goal is to find clues in other symptoms to the reasons behind her crying. **Remember: It is the other symptoms associated with the crying that lead us to the illness, and not just the crying itself.**

So ask yourself:

- ❖ Has your child been sick with anything else?
- ❖ Has she had diarrhea?
- ❖ Is she vomiting?
- ❖ Does she have cold symptoms?
- ❖ Does she have a fever?
- ❖ Has she had a bowel movement in the last two days?

One of the most common causes of crying in babies is an **ear infection.** They cry from the discomfort. The signs may be subtle: cold symptoms, a runny nose, perhaps even a little diarrhea or vomiting, a low-grade fever. Often we will need to see a child to diagnose ear infections, because sometimes the symptoms are so subtle that only an examination will tell. There are many times I've had a kid brought in to my office, and I could have sworn that she had gas. When I examined her, there was an ear infection clear as day.

Ear infections are a common cause of unexplained crying in babies. Their ears really hurt from the infection, but they can't tell us what the problem is, so they cry. Lying down can increase or trigger the crying. Persistent unexplained crying in an infant is often worth a trip to the doctor's office to check for ear infection.

Little babies also get **sore throats** just as do their older brothers and sisters.

Abdominal pain and **stomach cramps** can also make a young baby cry. Every parent's fear is that their child will develop appendicitis. So endless crying, especially if she seems to have abdominal distress, can make parents especially anxious. Children under six months very rarely get appendicitis. It does happen, though. So you should be on the lookout for a kid who won't stop crying, even when treated with the standard colic remedies like snugglies, rocking, going outdoors or going for a ride in the car.

Vomiting and diarrhea are more common signs that she has a **viral illness.** You should be even more suspicious if you or your other children have also had these symptoms. Generally, in a very young child, I'd still suggest that you contact your doctor just to be sure.

Sometimes, as with Sherlock Holmes, the clue is in what isn't there. Very young babies can get constipated, often without the parents realizing that days have gone by and the child hasn't had a bowel movement. I find this often happens in a household where both parents work; both the parents and the care-giver or day-care center assume that the bowel movement has taken place on the other's watch. For this reason, many good day-care centers will give parents a daily briefing on kids' bowel habits. If you suspect constipation in your little baby, read the chapter on constipation.

By far the most common and most troublesome cause of infant crying is **colic.**

What is colic? Colic is usually a diagnosis of exclusion. In other words, after we exclude all other possibilities, we conclude that the crying is caused by colic. If there is no ear infection, no fever, no vomiting, no diarrhea and no rash and yet the crying persists, we presume it is colic.

No one knows exactly what colic is. It is thought to have something to do with the digestive system. One possibility is that it is related to a reaction to cow milk and cow milk products. Sometimes mothers find that by eliminating cow milk from their babies' diets, or from their own diets if they are nursing, they can substantially reduce the crying bouts.

But in other cases, we can find no clear cause. We define colic, then, as severe bouts of crying that last for hours at a time, and from which the baby is not easily distracted. But even a colicky baby can be distracted from crying by walking, or getting dressed and going outside.

Even with severe cases of colic, there are things that you can do that will often have some effect. Car rides are among the most popular solutions. There is something about the motion of the car that appears to soothe a colicky baby. Sometimes parents at their wit's end will just pile everyone in the car and drive aimlessly around for the chance to have a half hour or so of peace and quiet.

If that's not possible, or if you're city-bound or don't have a car, other people claim that setting the kid in a baby seat on top of the clothes dryer has the same effect. There are even companies that sell little vibrating machines that mimic the rocking motion of a car or a dryer that the company claims will calm down colicky babies.

I've found that clothes dryers and walking about indoors do have some effect, but not as much as going outdoors. There's something about the outdoors that adds to the soothing effect. In fact, when I get a frantic call from a mother going into her sixth hour with a crying baby, my first suggestion, even in the dead of winter, is to go out for a walk with the baby in the snuggly.

Some parents have found that it helps to put pressure on the child's stomach. Carrying the baby in a football position with your hand on her stomach, or slung over your shoulder with her tummy on your shoulder, may give the baby—and you—some relief.

Still, colic can easily exhaust all parents' resources because it requires their complete attention and effort to keep the baby from crying. As long as you are walking around holding him in the snuggly (preferably outdoors) or riding in the car, he's fine. The second you stop, he's crying again.

Some people say that simethacone drops, which are an anti-gas preparation, give kids comfort and parents peace. I have never found them to be of any great use, but I wouldn't quarrel with anything safe that parents find to be helpful. In the end, my only word of comfort for parents who find that nothing much works is that colic doesn't last forever. You will wake up one morning when your child is two or three months old and discover that it's all over.

Teething is another possible cause of crying in a young baby. In its earliest stages, it begins with the baby rubbing his mouth and drooling. That begins as early as three to four months of age. Teething doesn't usually appear to cause children real discomfort until six to eight months of age when the teeth really begin to work their way through the gums. The discomfort of teething can persist until all the baby teeth have broken through at about 18 months old. Even though parents often call their doctors for advice about teething, it helps to remember that teething isn't an illness. It's a normal part of a child's development. No special treatment is necessary.

Parents are, of course, concerned about their child's comfort. There have been all sorts of remedies proposed over the years, from giving frozen teething rings to rubbing whiskey on the gums. There are also local anesthetics (available at drug stores) that supposedly give some relief. My experience is that, while any of these remedies may give some spot relief for a few minutes, none of them provides any long-term help. In fact, none is really needed. You'll watch your child herself gnaw on her fist, which is her way of seeking comfort. During the day, I find that most babies do this to distract themselves from the discomfort.

If, on the other hand, you find that nighttime is difficult for you and the baby, try whatever you can to relieve her discomfort. In my experience, if she seems really uncomfortable, which usually happens just as the teeth are actually erupting, then some acetaminophen just before bed seems to work as well as anything else.

CHECKLIST

HEADACHE:

WITH FEVER, DIARRHEA OR VOMITING: Consider viral illness.

AFTER EATING A PARTICULAR FOOD: Consider food intolerance.

DURING OR AFTER SOME UPSETTING TIME: Consider stress or tension.

WITH FEVER, VOMITING AND STIFF NECK: Consider meningitis. Consult your physician immediately.

WITH SENSITIVITY TO LIGHT, SMELLS OR FOOD: Consider migraine.

NECK PAIN:

WHERE NECK IS PAINFUL TO MOVE FORWARD TOWARD THE CHEST (USUALLY ACCOMPANIED BY FEVER AND VOMITING): Consider meningitis. Consult physician immediately.

WHERE NECK IS PAINFUL TO MOVE FROM SIDE TO SIDE: With cold or flu symptoms, consider viral illness. Consult physician.

WITH SWOLLEN NECK GLANDS AND POSSIBLY FEVER: Consider a throat infection (pharyngitis).

STOMACH ACHE:

CONTINUAL STOMACH PAIN THAT INCREASES OVER TIME: Consider appendicitis. Check for signs of appendicitis: pain at the midpoint of the abdomen, between the belly button and the right side; a characteristic posture, lying down with legs drawn up; pain that builds and does not diminish. Consult physician immediately.

ACUTE STOMACH PAIN THAT IS RELIEVED BY VOMITING (OFTEN ACCOMPANIED BY FEVER): Consider viral illness.

CRAMPING OR FEELING BLOATED: After a long interval between bowel movements. Consider constipation. Read constipation chapter. Try home remedies.

CRAMPING OR ACUTE FLU-LIKE STOMACH PAIN THAT RECURS: Consider food allergy or food intolerance. Identify and remove offending food.

ACUTE CRAMPY PAINS: Consider gas. Wait to see if pain is relieved by passing gas. If pain is not relieved within an hour or two, consider appendicitis.

PAIN IN THE LOWER BACK, WITH HIGH FEVER: Consider kidney infection. Consult physician immediately.

STOMACH PAIN (WITHOUT OTHER SYMPTOMS) ASSOCIATED WITH EVENTS LIKE SCHOOL: Consider stress or fears.

PAIN IN THE LEGS:

LEG PAINS AT NIGHT OR WHILE RESTING: Consider growing pains. These pains respond to massaging, hot baths or acetaminophen.

LEG PAIN IN ONE SPECIFIC SPOT THAT DOESN'T CHANGE: If there has been any trauma, a hit or a fall, consider a fracture. Consult your physician promptly.

PAIN IN THE JOINTS:

JOINT PAIN WITH LOW-GRADE FEVER, STOMACH UPSET OR COLD SYMPTOMS: Consider viral illness. Try home remedies (see fever section).

JOINT PAIN FOLLOWING A TICK BITE, AND FOLLOWING A FEVER AND A BULL'S-EYE RASH: Consider Lyme disease. Consult your physician.

JOINT PAIN IN ONE SPECIFIC JOINT FOLLOWING A BLOW OR A FALL: Consider trauma. Immobilize the joint, help the child rest. Consult physician if discomfort persists.

ELBOW PAIN FOLLOWING A TUG OR JERK ON THE ARM: If the child refuses to move his arm, consider nursemaid's elbow. Try home remedy described above. If unsuccessful, consult physician. Follow with acetaminophen and warm compresses if necessary.

ONGOING JOINT PAIN COMBINED WITH JOINT SWELLING: In joint pain for which there is no other explanation, consult your physician for a possible consideration of rheumatoid arthritis.

CHEST PAIN:

CHEST PAIN WITH COUGH, FEVER AND BREATHING DIFFICULTY: Consider pneumonia. Consult your physician immediately.

CHEST PAIN ACCOMPANYING VIRAL ILLNESS AND COUGH: Consider pulled muscle. This pain should go away in a couple of days by itself.

PERSISTENT CHEST PAIN: Accompanied by lethargy, loss of appetite, general appearance of ill health. Generally in older children and adolescents. Consider myocarditis, although it is rare. Consult your physician.

EAR PAIN:

WITH COLD SYMPTOMS: Consider ear infection. Other typical signs are poor sleeping, fussiness, decreased appetite and diarrhea. Consult physician.

AFTER SWIMMING WITH OUTER EAR THAT IS PAINFUL TO THE TOUCH: Consider swimmer's ear. Consult physician.

IN ONE EAR WITHOUT OTHER SYMPTOMS: Consider object in ear. Investigate the circumstances. Consult physician.

SEVERE PAIN THAT SUDDENLY STOPS: Suspect a ruptured ear drum and consult the doctor.

SORE THROAT:

IN THE SUMMER: Consider allergies. Consult your physician who may prescribe antihistamines.

IN THE WINTER OFTEN ACCOMPANIED BY COUGH, RUNNY NOSE AND STUFFINESS: Consider viral illness.

ACCOMPANIED BY FEVER: Consider strep throat. Consult your physician who will prescribe antibiotics.

REPEATED SORE THROAT IN A HOUSEHOLD WHERE THERE ARE SMOKERS: Consider smokers' cough. The solution: quit smoking.

EYE PAIN:

ACCOMPANIED BY REDNESS IN BOTH EYES: Suspect conjunctivitis (pinkeye). Read "Eyes" chapter. Consult physician.

ASSOCIATED WITH DIRT OR DUST IN EYE: Flush out eye. Observe child. If discomfort persists, consider corneal abrasion and consult physician.

FOLLOWING STRIKE OR BLOW: Suspect trauma. Observe child. If child appears in great discomfort, or refuses to remove his hand from his eye, consult physician immediately.

WITH COLD SYMPTOMS (LIKE RUNNY NOSE, OR CONGESTION OR A COUGH, ESPECIALLY AT NIGHT): Consider sinusitis. Consult physician. Use acetaminophen or a decongestant to relieve the pain.

WITH NO OTHER SYMPTOMS: Consider early stages of other illness like flu or infectious mononucleosis. Read "Fever" chapter, check for other symptoms.

RECTAL PAIN:

FOLLOWING PASSAGE OF A HARD STOOL: Consider irritation from constipation. Read "Constipation" chapter, treat the constipation and apply petroleum-based ointment locally to ease discomfort.

FOLLOWING DIARRHEA: Consider irritation. Read "Diarrhea" chapter. Treat the diarrhea and apply petroleum-based ointment locally to ease discomfort.

RECTAL ITCHING OR DISCOMFORT: Possibly accompanied by stomach ache. Consider infection with pinworms. Consult physician.

ASSOCIATED WITH BEHAVIORAL CHANGES (LIKE BED-WETTING, UNUSUAL FEARS, ANXIETY OR DEPRESSION): Consider sexual abuse. Consult your physician who will refer you to a professional child abuse team.

PAIN ON URINATION:

WITHOUT FEVER: Consider irritated urethra. Try warm non-soapy baths or local cream to reduce the irritation. Consult physician if condition persists or if fever develops.

WITH LOW FEVER: Consider urinary tract infection. Consult physician.

WITH HIGH SPIKING FEVER: Consider kidney infection. Consult physician immediately.

ACCOMPANIED BY BEHAVIORAL CHANGES (LIKE BED-WETTING, UNUSUAL FEARS, ANXIETY OR DEPRESSION): Consider sexual abuse. Consult your physician who will refer you to a professional child abuse team.

MOUTH PAIN:

PAIN FROM CUTS IN THE MOUTH: Consult physician if bleeding doesn't stop promptly.

PAIN FROM CUTS ON THE TONGUE: Consult physician. Cuts on the tongue can require stitches.

PAIN FROM MOUTH SORES: Consider viruses. Treat with acetaminophen until the sores subside.

PAIN FROM MOUTH RASHES ASSOCIATED WITH FOODS: Consider allergies. Identify and remove the offending food.

MOUTH PAIN ASSOCIATED WITH TEETHING: Relieve discomfort with acetaminophen.

UNEXPLAINED CRYING:

Here are a few of the more common causes for crying that goes on and on:

EAR INFECTION: Possibly associated with cold symptoms.

TEETHING: In babies from 4 to 18 months.

SORE THROAT: Possibly associated with cold symptoms.

GAS PAIN: This should go away by itself when the child passes gas.

IN THE MIDDLE OF THE NIGHT: Consider nightmares or night terrors. Comfort the child, or try taking her outdoors.

COLIC: This crying can often be relieved by going outdoors or by riding in the car.

HAIR TOURNIQUET SYNDROME: Check your child's fingers or toes carefully because a piece of hair can become wrapped tightly around digits and cause swelling and pain.

SHALL I WAKE THE DOCTOR?

Here are the conditions that would warrant a midnight call to your doctor, or a midnight rush to the emergency room:

ANY PAIN WITH HIGH FEVER: This could signify any of a number of serious conditions like meningitis or kidney infection, or pneumonia. Your doctor may decide to respond with the standard fever treatment—acetaminophen and a cool bath to bring the fever down. But because of the possibilities of something more serious, you should at least check.

PROLONGED CRYING WITH ABDOMINAL PAIN: This means a really unhappy child who cries for more than an hour without letup. This still may signify nothing more than a virus or gas, or colic in a baby. But it could also signify appendicitis.

HIGH FEVER AND PAIN ON URINATION: This could signify a kidney infection.

BACK PAIN WITH HIGH FEVER: This could also signify a kidney infection.

SEVERE HEADACHE WITH FEVER AND VOMITING: This could mean meningitis.

STIFF NECK WITH FEVER AND VOMITING: This could also mean meningitis.

EYE PAIN: If there has been some trauma to the eye.

DIARRHEA

In one big city emergency room there is a sophisticated diagnostic tool we use to determine if a sick child needs immediate attention or can wait his turn. We call it the Cheese Doodles Test. We offer the sick kid a bag of Cheese Doodles from one of the vending machines in the lobby and watch what happens. The child who digs right in—despite his complaints and his parents' worries—goes to the end of the line.

We don't always actually use Cheese Doodles of course. But the idea of the test is diagnostic. With diarrhea as with most other childhood conditions, the most important thing to watch is the child's behavior. A parent can assume that even a child who is miserable with diarrhea, vomiting and fever is probably going to be okay if he will eat chips and drink soda.

That is not to say that diarrhea isn't a serious condition. It is. Up until the 20th century, diarrhea was a major killer of children everywhere in the world; in underdeveloped countries, it still is. Modern sanitation and clean water supplies have eliminated that danger for most children in industrialized countries, though. The danger of diarrhea, however, isn't the condition itself; it is the dehydration that can follow when a child loses fluids continuously over a long period of time.

So the important task for parents with a child who has diarrhea is to manage the diarrhea to make sure that the child doesn't lose too much fluid. The benchmark parents can use for both tasks takes us right back to the Cheese Doodles Test: It's behavior, including the child's willingness to eat and drink, that is the most important thing for a parent to watch. It will give us clues as to both the cause and the severity of the illness, and help us understand if the condition is serious or likely to pass on its own.

How do you know if your child is getting enough fluid? By his behavior. If your child accepts fluids and even small amounts of food, and continues to show interest in his normal activities, chances are you'll make it through this episode without even a visit to the doctor. I handle the vast majority of calls I get for diarrhea over the phone. Usually dietary management alone is sufficient.

Whatever the cause of diarrhea, be alert to the possibility of dehydration. I'll discuss dehydration, its symptoms and its prevention later in the chapter.

EVALUATING DIARRHEA

Here are some questions to ask yourself:

❖ What is the frequency and consistency of your child's stools?
❖ Is your child vomiting as well?
❖ Does he have a fever?
❖ Is he active or lethargic?
❖ Is the child urinating normally?
❖ Will he drink fluids?
❖ Will he eat?
❖ How long have his loose stools persisted?
❖ Does an anti-diarrhea diet help?
❖ Has the child eaten anything unusual or suspicious recently?

❖ Does the diarrhea seem to be associated with any particular food?

❖ Is the child also tugging at his ear, or complaining of ear pain?

Parents usually wonder if their child actually has diarrhea. Most doctors figure that during your child's first three years of life, he will experience from one to three acute episodes of diarrhea. Our definition of diarrhea is simply bowel movements that are more loose, frequent and watery than usual. Any bowel movements that are looser than normal qualify as diarrhea. In a breast-fed baby, whose stools are normally very loose, diarrhea would make the stools practically liquid. In an older child the stools will be looser than normal and may change in color or smell. In any case, the volume of feces increases considerably in a child with diarrhea. As a parent, you'll know your own child's bowel habits, and will notice the changes.

Diarrhea may range from mild to severe. When diarrhea is severe, a child may have many bowel movements in a day and the stools may be quite liquid, whatever the child's age.

If there is vomiting, often a parent will notice the vomiting before the diarrhea. In a typical case, the child will begin vomiting and have a fever. Then about 24 hours later, the diarrhea will begin. In such a case, I would suspect a viral infection.

Viral infections are the major cause of diarrhea in children. Like most viruses, cases of diarrhea come in packs, sort of like little epidemics. I will go for weeks at a time with only an occasional call about diarrhea. Then, suddenly, I'll receive five calls a day. As a parent, you may notice the same thing. You'll hear about diarrhea at school, at the day-care center, on the playground. This is the kind of viral infection you'll call a stomach flu.

Severe diarrhea (that is, many liquid stools in a day) should last only a day or so. The whole attack of diarrhea that is caused by a virus should usually last no more than a few days. Your child may vomit several times, and have frequent, loose, often smelly bowel movements. He may be uncomfortable and complain of stomach ache. But he should be alert and comfortable enough to want to play with his favorite toys, or watch a video. While he may appear sick and not as perky as usual, he shouldn't appear droopy and lethargic, nor persistently refuse his favorite activities or foods. In fact, your problem may be in temporarily refusing his favorite foods in the interest of halting the diarrhea attack.

Read the section on dietary management. Follow it. If the severe diarrhea persists for longer than one day, or the entire attack doesn't clear up by itself within a few days, consult your doctor to see if some other factor is at work.

VERY SEVERE DIARRHEA OR DIARRHEA THAT PERSISTS

Very, severe diarrhea is diarrhea that involves many liquid stools a day for longer than a single day. Viral infections can be really severe on the first day, but they tend to begin to clear up after the first 24 hours. If the diarrhea doesn't ease up after the first 24 hours, call your doctor. Violent diarrhea can be caused by **food poisoning,** which comes from getting a bacterial infection. The most common bacteria are salmonella or staphylococcus. If a number of people break out with similar acute symptoms in a similar time period, we may want to test stools to try to find out what was responsible, if only to try to prevent others from becoming ill. But most of the time it isn't important to try to find out the cause, because the treatment is going to be the same in either case.

You can consider some form of food poisoning during the first 24 hours if you think that your child has eaten something that might be carrying bacteria. Some common culprits are raw eggs and raw chicken—transmitters of salmonella—and any kind of spoiled food in which staphylococcal bacteria can thrive.

Food poisoning does require a little bit more parental attention, but usually only because the diarrhea is more severe, and thus dehydration is more likely. But the basic treatment is still dietary management.

One other possible cause of persistent or severe diarrhea that does require a different form of treatment is **giardia.** This is a parasite transmitted by feces. School-age children are subject to giardia, since it is passed from person to person via less than perfect hygiene practices. It can also come from drinking contaminated water. If you have just returned from camping when the symptoms crop up, you might suspect giardia.

One other clue is that giardia usually will cause long-lasting diarrhea and stomach pain and cramps, but won't cause any other symptoms like vomiting or fever. In this case, call your doctor; he or she may want to do a stool culture to test for the presence of this parasite. The treatment in this case consists of anti-parasite medication.

DIARRHEA WITH A FEVER

Usually fever with diarrhea is just one more sign that the child is suffering from a viral infection. There can be other causes, though.

Oddly enough, persistent diarrhea can be a sign of **ear infection** or **urinary tract infection.** So if your child has diarrhea with a fever that persists even after you try the dietary management techniques I describe later, look for other signs that your child might be suffering from an ear or urinary tract infection. In a younger child, say around two years old, you will see poor sleeping, fussiness and a decreased appetite, possibly combined with an intermittent fever. Be particularly suspicious if these symptoms follow a cold. In older kids, the symptoms will be even more specific, as they will often complain of an earache. On the other hand urinary tract infections in young kids can occur without really specific symptoms, so if diarrhea persists with an intermittent fever, call your physician to discuss the possibility of a urinary tract or an ear infection.

PERSISTENT DIARRHEA WITH NO OTHER SYMPTOMS

If your child's diarrhea persists for longer than a week, in spite of dietary management, and with no other symptoms like a fever or vomiting you should consider **food intolerance.** Children can get diarrhea from a wide range of foods. But the most common food intolerance is **lactose intolerance.** Lactose is the sugar found in cow milk and cow milk products. Children with lactose intolerance lack a certain enzyme that helps break down lactose, which is found in cow milk and products like yogurt and cheese. It is an extremely common problem. In some ethnic groups it is more common than others. People of Asian or African heritage are more likely than other groups to be lactose intolerant. Lactose intolerance causes diarrhea when the undigested lactose passes through the system and irritates it, sometimes causing cramping. This condition can be present in a newborn, or develop any time later in life. It can be temporary, or a permanent condition. It can often follow an episode of viral diarrhea.

DIARRHEA WHILE TRAVELING

Unfortunately, children are just as vulnerable to Montezuma's revenge as adults are—maybe even more so, since their intestines aren't acclimated to as wide a range of bacteria. So don't be surprised if your trip is accompanied by a bout of diarrhea in your child.

One type of traveler's diarrhea comes from contact with strains of bacteria that are simply different than the ones they are accustomed to. The new set of bacteria colonize the intestines and, in doing so, cause loose stools. A child can be subject to this kind of diarrhea in travelling almost anywhere, even to Aunt Rose's. Usually this kind of diarrhea is mild, and corrects itself within a couple of days after returning home.

The other type is the more serious traveler's diarrhea. It comes from exposure to the kinds of bacteria—like salmonella—we discussed earlier. When travelling to places where sanitary food preparation is less reliable and the water supply not necessarily pure, a parent's major job is to try to prevent traveler's diarrhea. All the usual travelling precautions must be taken: drinking only bottled water; using only bottled or boiled water for teeth brushing; avoiding unpeeled fresh fruit and vegetables. For little babies the standards should be even more rigorous. Some parents try to carry everything with them—baby food, formula, water—rather than trusting local preparations.

If a child does contract traveler's diarrhea, it's important to practice the dietary management that I'll discuss later, to watch the severity of the diarrhea, and to prevent dehydration by giving the child sufficient fluids. Of course you have to be sure that the fluids you are giving the child are pure and not contributing to the problem. Stick with bottled water or canned or bottled fruit juices.

BLOOD IN THE STOOL

Blood in the stool is usually a much less serious sign than parents think it is. If a child has had diarrhea for a while, the stools can often show streaks of blood. While that appears frightening, it is almost always from superficial irritation of the rectal area.

Parents should make a distinction between a few little blood streaks, which are harmless, and bloody stools, which are not. **Irritation in the rectum** will cause thread-like streaks of fresh blood that don't appear to be part of the stool itself. With bloody stools, the stool itself is mixed with blood.

The most serious example of that is what we call **currant jelly stools,** where there is a lot of blood mixed in with the stool. The name comes from the color of the stool; because the blood has entered into the stool higher up in the digestive system, it doesn't look like fresh blood, but rather has a darker, more purplish cast to it. That kind of bloody stool is a sign of **intussusception,** which is a very serious condition.

I see this condition about once or twice a year in my practice. It occurs when one section of the intestine telescopes into another. It causes severe intestinal pain which leads us to suspect such serious conditions as appendicitis, an intestinal infection or intussusception. Currant jelly stools with or without abdominal pain is a severe symptom and requires immediate medical attention.

DEHYDRATION

In nearly every case of diarrhea, no matter what the cause, the thing I have warned parents to worry about the most is **dehydration.**

Here's what parents need to watch out for:

- ❖ Severe diarrhea that lasts longer than a day or two
- ❖ A child who refuses to eat or drink
- ❖ A child who is willing to eat or drink but is vomiting for more than a day.
- ❖ A normally active child who becomes lethargic, whiny or crying
- ❖ A child who goes longer than eight hours without urinating
- ❖ Dry mouth
- ❖ No tears

A parent who notices any or all of these symptoms should call the physician immediately. These symptoms could indicate that the diarrhea is leading to dehydration that you can't simply treat at home.

It isn't uncommon for a child with diarrhea to develop mild dehydration. Such a child will be more thirsty than usual. This is a condition that requires good dietary management that I will discuss later. It isn't a medical emergency. Only if the diarrhea continues and the dehydration progresses to a moderate state will we become really concerned—perhaps enough to bring the child in for examination and possible hospital treatment with intravenous fluid administration. Moderate dehydration is less common. Still, all parents should be aware of the symptoms, and alert to the possibility.

If the child is beginning to **refuse fluids,** that's a reason to call the doctor for an assessment. With mild dehydration, thirst increases as the body demands to replace the fluids it's lost. But as the dehydration becomes more severe, irritability sets in and the child refuses to drink. A dehydrated child will have less saliva than normal. Feel his mouth to see if it is dry. Compare it to your own.

Another sign is a **cessation of urination.** The exact time period can vary from child to child. You will know your own child's pattern of urination and can notice any variation from that. It isn't unusual for a child with diarrhea to go six hours without urinating. But a general benchmark that I would use is that a child should urinate or wet at least one diaper in eight hours. If in doubt, call the doctor and check it out.

Another sign is **lethargy, fatigue or crying.** A child with garden-variety viral diarrhea is uncomfortable, but not usually sick enough to be really miserable. Your child with diarrhea may be mopey and less energetic than usual, and may complain of a stomach ache. But he should show some interest in his toys and his cartoons, or a game of Old Maid. He shouldn't really be weepy either. If a child with diarrhea who doesn't usually cry a lot begins to cry continually, that's not a good sign, especially if he isn't producing any tears. **Absence of tears** is another sign of dehydration. Call the doctor.

We are generally more concerned about dehydration in younger children than in older children, because a one-year-old has smaller fluid reserves than a 12-year-old. In general, the younger the child, the more concerned we are.

DIETARY MANAGEMENT OF DIARRHEA

The most important thing to do in handling diarrhea is what we call **dietary management.** First, we try to replace the fluids the child is losing. Second, we switch him temporarily to a diet that helps to reduce the frequency of the diarrhea and solidify the stools.

Only after the diarrhea has stabilized do we begin to reintroduce normal foods.

The best thing for replacing fluids in a child with vomiting and diarrhea is an electrolyte solution. These solutions are specially designed to replace not only water lost in vomiting and diarrhea, but also the lost salts, or electrolytes. These solutions can be bought in drug stores or supermarkets under brand names such as Pedialyte or Ricelyte.

The problem is that even the flavored solutions don't taste great (they're salty) and very young kids may refuse them for that reason alone. So I often suggest to parents that they turn to another kind of electrolyte solution: the sports drink. These drinks, like Gatorade, are also designed to prevent dehydration in athletic adults. They tend to be sweeter, and thus more palatable to kids. Because they are so concentrated, though, it is important to dilute with equal parts of water.

But if your kid refuses even Gatorade, just about anything will do. Coca-Cola or ginger ale is fine. I suggest letting it get a bit flat first, though, since the gas bubbles can irritate an already sensitive stomach. Apple juice (diluted with water so that it isn't too sweet) or even plain water will do the trick.

The main thing you *shouldn't* give your child who is vomiting or has diarrhea is milk. I can't count how many calls like this I've had from panicky parents:

> "He seemed better. He even drank down his whole bottle
> of milk, and then up it came again and his diarrhea has
> come back."

Sensitive stomachs are irritated by milk, so avoid it. What's more, as I discussed earlier, milk may actually be a cause of the diarrhea itself. Even kids who aren't normally lactose intolerant can sometimes develop a temporary lactose intolerance following a bout of diarrhea.

As far as managing the diarrhea attack itself, here's the important thing to remember: Clear liquids only for the first 12 to 24 hours. If your child wants ice cream or Pop Tarts (or Cheese Doodles!), that's tough. Here's where you have to be firm. If you want the diarrhea to go away, stick to this rule.

Of course, many parents just aren't that disciplined or hard-hearted. And many kids just aren't that sick. Giving a kid with diarrhea his favorite food isn't going to hurt him. It may, however, prolong the bout of diarrhea. It's only with infants that we doctors are very firm about enforcing a clear liquids-only diet at the beginning of diarrhea.

The best course of treatment for an older child—that is one over six months old—is an initial 24-hour period of liquids only, followed by a day or so of what we call the BRAT diet. Now you may have your own ideas about why we call it that. But actually, it's just an acronym for the foods that we have found help bind the stools and slow down diarrhea: bananas, rice, applesauce and toast. Luckily, these are foods that kids usually find pretty tolerable.

So by the second day of the diarrhea, if your child has shown that he can hold down liquids, begin offering him some bananas—mashed if he is still a toddler—and some applesauce. Keep the toast plain if you can, although a smear of jelly won't hurt. Then if your child tolerates these foods well, you can gradually reintroduce other foods a day later, remembering that his appetite may be down and his stomach sensitive after his bout with diarrhea.

Remember, too, that these are general guidelines for a model situation. Most situations aren't model situations and few kids I've seen have been model kids. If your kid is absolutely shrieking for Chicken McNuggets, try it—but beware the consequences!

MEDICATION FOR DIARRHEA

Travelers have long known that there are two fairly effective medications for diarrhea. Either Pepto-Bismol, or Kaopectate are safe medications that will reduce the severity and duration of a diarrhea attack. I don't generally recommend medication for diarrhea, since it is usually a self-limiting condition. But now and then other physicians may recommend one of these medications, or a newer one called Immodium, if they feel that the diarrhea itself is causing enough irritation to be a problem. In this case, the irritable bowel will itself be a cause of diarrhea, and a vicious cycle will be established. If dietary management alone isn't enough to break this vicious cycle, then you might want to consult your doctor about using one of these medications. One caution though: Another popular traveler's medication, Lomotil, isn't suitable for children under 12 years old.

YOUR CHILD UNDER SIX MONTHS

Any of the symptoms and conditions we have already talked about can occur in children under six months. The only possible exception is intussuception, which is not common in very little babies.

The important thing for parents of infants to remember is that they should be much more alert than parents of older children. Tiny babies become dehydrated much faster than do older children because their fluid reserves are that much smaller. The smaller the baby, the quicker he can become dehydrated. That's why infants are more likely to be hospitalized for intravenous fluids than are older children. Little babies can develop a vicious cycle of vomiting and diarrhea and become dehydrated quickly.

The oral electrolyte solutions I discussed earlier are a breakthrough in treatment and are very effective in treating babies, who don't seem to object to the salty taste as much as older children do. But don't try treating vomiting and diarrhea in a child under six months on your own. Call your doctor. He or she may want to examine him or even hospitalize him for a course of intravenous fluids.

CHECKLIST

DIARRHEA:

LOOSE STOOLS, INCREASED FREQUENCY, CHANGE IN COLOR OR ODOR OF STOOLS (MAY ALSO BE ACCOMPANIED BY VOMITING AND FEVER): Consider viral infection. Practice dietary management, and observe child for dehydration.

SEVERE OR VIOLENT DIARRHEA (MANY LIQUID STOOLS THAT PERSIST FOR LONGER THAN ONE DAY): Consider bacterial infection like food poisoning. Call your doctor.

PERSISTENT DIARRHEA WITH A FEVER: Consider ear infection or urinary tract infection. Consult physician.

PERSISTENT DIARRHEA WITH NO OTHER SYMPTOMS: Consider food intolerance.

DIARRHEA WHEN TRAVELLING: Practice dietary management and observe child for possible dehydration.

STREAKS OF BLOOD IN THE STOOLS: Consider irritation of rectal area. Observe child.

DARK RED BLOOD MIXED WITH STOOL AND ABDOMINAL PAIN: Consider intussusception and contact physician immediately. This is a serious condition.

IF YOUR CHILD WITH DIARRHEA REFUSES FLUIDS, BECOMES LETHARGIC, WEEPY, OR WHINY, ACTS FATIGUED, HAS A DRY MOUTH, CRIES WITHOUT TEARS: Consider dehydration. Consult physician promptly. This is a serious condition.

SHALL I WAKE THE DOCTOR?

You should seek emergency treatment immediately for **bloody diarrhea.** That means stools with a large quantity of real blood, not just small bloody streaks.

You also shouldn't hesitate to wake your doctor if your child has **diarrhea and a high temperature.** (Use over 105° as a rough guideline.) That combination could be the sign of a serious intestinal infection.

Even without a fever, you should call your doctor day or night for any child who has diarrhea and is **lethargic and refusing to drink.** The child may be so dehydrated as to require a trip to the emergency room for intravenous fluids.

Diarrhea with severe abdominal cramps should also be observed by a doctor immediately. That doesn't mean the passing five and ten-minute cramps that often accompany the kind of diarrhea kids get when they have an intestinal virus. That means a pain that persists for more than an hour. In an older child, it might be a pain that prevents him from walking. In a younger child, it would be a pain that leads to prolonged crying. This could possibly signal appendicitis.

In babies under six months, I would expect to be awakened for any **diarrhea accompanied by fever.** In this case—as is always the case with tiny babies—it is the fever that is important.

WHEN CAN HE GO BACK TO SCHOOL?

As much as anything else, common sense governs the return to school of a child with diarrhea. Generally we don't need to worry much about contagion once any fever has been down for 24 hours. But even without a fever, any child who has diarrhea severe or frequent enough to require dietary management should be kept out of school. It's only logical. A child with diarrhea wants nothing more than quick and easy access to a bathroom—and a change of clothing if things go wrong. Be fair to the child and to his teachers. Keep him home until the diarrhea is under control.

ASK DR. JOHN

QUESTION: I've heard that we shouldn't treat diarrhea since it's the body's way of cleansing itself out. Is that true?

ANSWER: Diarrhea is an illness, the result of the body's reaction to an infection. We treat diarrhea because the possibility of dehydration far outweighs any possible "cleansing" effect it has.

QUESTION: My child had diarrhea and seemed to be recovered so I gave him his bottle. He threw it up, and I noticed it was curdled. Is it possible the milk is bad? Is that what made him sick in the first place?

ANSWER: I doubt it. Curdling is a normal part of digestion. Intolerance for milk following a bout with diarrhea is very common. Children develop temporary lactose intolerance. That's why I suggest that parents give fruit juice, flat soft drinks, electrolyte solutions or just plain water to kids recovering from diarrhea and skip the milk altogether for a couple of days.

QUESTION: My child had diarrhea, but then all of a sudden the color of his stools changed to a greenish color with a very foul smell. Doesn't this mean that he's gotten sicker?

ANSWER: No. The color of the stool is only significant if it indicates a significant quantity of blood. The color variants are usually the result of how quickly food is passing through the system. The same is true for the characteristic foul smell of the stool.

QUESTION: Where do children get these things?

ANSWER: Blame their little friends, or your parents, or the last guest you had for dinner or just about anyone. The viruses that cause diarrhea and vomiting are passed from person to person. Young kids, who haven't yet built up immunity to the ranges of viruses out there, will tend to be more susceptible.

QUESTION: Can I do anything to prevent it?

ANSWER: No. Diarrhea is just part of the natural order of things. Until the young child's body develops antibodies, he's going to get sick. Getting sick, in fact, is one way that he does develop the antibodies that will protect him later on. There aren't any vaccines yet for stomach flu.

EARS

All kids get ear infections.

That's one thing I can say with as much certainty as I can say that all people get colds. The reason I can be so certain is that in kids, colds and ear infections go hand-in-hand. Of course, most kids will make it through most colds without having an ear infection. But sooner or later all parents will have to grapple with at least one ear infection. And for some children, ear infections will be so common that their parents will become expert enough to treat these episodes as almost routine events.

Obviously there are other reasons for ear pain in children, including the possibility that they have managed to lodge some object in their ear. We will discuss how to check on that possibility, and what to do about it later. Still, it is pretty easy to distinguish between the two causes, since ear infections usually begin when a child has a cold or sinus infection.

While some kids seem to be especially susceptible to ear infections, the cause isn't usually related to their overall level of health. It's almost always just the plumbing. While doctors haven't always agreed about what causes ear infections, the current theory is that it has to do with the eustachian tubes, the passages between the middle ear and the throat that allow fluid to drain from the ears.

Inside the external ear is an ear canal that leads to the eardrum. Behind the eardrum, towards the brain, there is the middle ear cavity, which has the little bones that conduct the vibrations from the eardrum and enable people to hear. That's the cavity that can be filled with fluid. That little cavity has a long thin tube leading to the back of the throat called the eustachian tube. At the opening of the eustachian tube in the back of the throat is the adenoid. In colds and sore throats, adenoids enlarge, blocking that eustachian tube off, and fluid fills up the middle ear space. Since there is always bacteria travelling up and down the eustachian tube, the fluid acts as a culture, and the bacteria cause an infection, creating both heat and pain.

The better developed the eustachian tubes, the more readily they drain. In kids in general the tubes are more immature than those of adults. And with some kids, parents will begin to notice that the child's one ear often becomes infected while the other is fine. I would suspect that the tubing on the bad side is just less developed than on the good side.

The good news is that the pipes grow along with the child. That means that even a child who for the first year or two had multiple ear infections will begin to have far fewer by the time he is three years old. By the time he reaches school age, the episodes should have dramatically reduced, if not vanished altogether.

In the meantime, ear infections are one of the leading reasons for wintertime visits to the pediatrician. I would recommend that you become familiar with the symptoms of ear infections that I am going to describe. Untreated ear infections can become very painful. Some people believe the speech of children who suffer extensively from ear infections may suffer because the fluid that builds up behind the eardrum can muffle sound and make it harder for a child just learning language to distinguish among words.

However, there's no scientific proof that the mild temporary hearing loss from ear infections can really disrupt language development. Nonetheless most doctors and parents choose to play it safe. Antibiotic treatment of ear infections is usually safe, easy to do and non-invasive. So in recent years, most doctors have opted for a pretty aggressive policy in treatment primarily because we'd like the child to be as comfortable as possible. So we like to try to catch ear infections early, and treat them promptly.

I would suggest that parents keep the possibility of ear infections in the back of their minds throughout the winter. While the outward symptoms of ear infections are often very clear and obvious, some children do develop ear infections that linger, nearly symptomless, for a long time. We sometimes find ear infections in children who have come to us to be evaluated for something else.

That's the bad news. The good news is that ear infections are very treatable.

When I see a child with a cold, I always check the eardrum for signs of infection. Some parents ask if they shouldn't get themselves the little tool with the light (an otoscope) so they themselves can check their child's ears. This is one area where I'd suggest parents depend on their doctors. Diagnosing ear infections is one of the trickiest jobs there is. I train interns to look for the signs of ear infections and I find that it is something they pick up only after long experience and much coaching. Even a parent with many children just isn't likely to get enough experience to reliably spot the signs. So I would suggest that parents become proficient in reading their child's other symptoms, but when necessary they should turn to their doctor for a more detailed diagnosis.

THE TUG

Here's a typical picture of the way an ear infection might look:

Your child has had a cold for several days, with a runny nose. The cold has been bad enough to make him uncomfortable, but not bad enough to keep him out of school. You had started to think he was getting over it, but today you've noticed that he's started to get weepy and cranky. He won't share his toys, and everything—from getting dressed to getting fed—is a major undertaking. Nothing seems right to him, and he cries and resists your every suggestion.

By bedtime you've noticed that he's running a little fever. What's more, he's clearly in pain now. Then the telltale sign appears: He begins to tug on his ear. In fact, he seems to be trying to get his hand into his ear. A bigger kid will often tell you outright, "Mommy, my ear hurts." But because the pain is inside the ear, it isn't always easy for a child to tell where the pain is coming from. So rather than verbalizing it, he will simply poke around in the general area, trying to put his fingers in his ears or fiddling with his neck or jaw under his earlobe.

One problem is that the older child, who is able to verbalize the problem, is also less likely to have an ear infection, since the frequency of ear infections decrease with age. Thus parents of younger children—six months to two years old—have to learn to read nonverbal clues. Even children who can speak clearly often have trouble finding the vocabulary for this type of pain, since it is internal and non-specific.

Also watch for sleeping problems and fussiness. The discomfort in the middle ear may express itself in nothing more than wakefulness and crankiness that can't be explained by any other cause.

A good eater who suddenly develops a bad appetite or diarrhea that doesn't seem to have any other cause should also be examined for an ear infection. We don't know why this is, but very often in young children ear infections seem to affect their digestive systems. If your child starts picking at his food and develops a mild case of diarrhea and a fever, of course you should first consider that he has an intenstinal flu. (Check the symptoms in the chapters on diarrhea and constipation.) But you should also be alert to the possibility that it might be an ear infection.

Sometimes the signs of an ear infection are truly clear-cut. A child with pressure building from an infection in his ear may be in a great deal of pain, howling, screaming and complaining that it hurts. I would suggest in this case that parents first try the treatment methods I will suggest later to relieve his discomfort. If you are one of the parents for whom an ear infection is a regular event, I would suggest that you immediately start him on the antibiotic that you and your doctor have decided is appropriate. But if the pain doesn't subside after treatment, by all means call the doctor, no matter what the hour. A child should not have to remain in that kind of pain all night.

What's more, severe pain may indicate that the fluid has built up behind the eardrum in sufficient quantities to threaten to rupture the eardrum itself. If the severe pain suddenly stops, and fluid begins running out of the ear, that indicates a **ruptured eardrum.**

In this case, the ear will be warm, or the child will have a fever. The wax from the inside of the ear will soften and run out, looking like a light yellowish pus. There will also be a discharge of a milky fluid, and perhaps some crusting, as the infected material from behind the eardrum drains away.

Most parents think a ruptured eardrum is a very scary and dangerous thing. Perhaps it's because they envision a toy drum with a big gash or a tear in it. But a ruptured eardrum in this day and age isn't usually a major problem. In fact, the rupture is usually just a tiny pinhole that opens and allows the painful fluid out. So for many children, the rupturing of an eardrum will cause an almost immediate relief from a big discomfort. Once the infection clears, the tiny hole then heals itself, leaving no long-term effects. In fact, in the days before the widespread use of antibiotics, pricking a hole in the eardrum (a myringotomy) was one of the accepted methods of treating a severe ear infection. The thing to remember is that the eardrum is tissue, just like the skin of your finger, and it heals in the same way.

While you shouldn't worry unduly, you should bring your child in during office hours to see the doctor. A small percentage of ruptured eardrums don't heal themselves and do require treatment by a specialist. What's more, although a perforation will relieve the pain, the child will still need antibiotics to clear the infection.

If your child has had repeated ear infections, and seems to be having trouble hearing, I would suggest having him examined and given a hearing test. In children who are too young to respond to the standard hearing tests, we can do a sophisticated measurement that shows whether or not the eardrum is registering sounds correctly and vibrating sufficiently.

While these days most ear infections are easily treated with antibiotics, sometimes kids with recurrent ear infections are put on a low dosage of antibiotic for the entire winter, simply as a preventative measure. Still, if your child's ear infections persist, and you and your doctor notice that fluid continually builds up behind your child's eardrum, causing pain and reduced hearing, you may want to consider another treatment approach.

In that case, the physician and parents may decide to have an ear, nose and throat doctor insert some plastic tubes to help the ear drain more completely.

Another possible cause of muffled hearing might be **serous otitis.** In this condition, fluid remains behind the eardrum even after infection has cleared. Again, the usual cause of this is simply the immaturity of the eustachian tubes. Since there is no infection, antibiotics won't help this condition. This is a chronic condition, so you and your pediatrician will have a lot of opportunity to discuss what to do. You too may decide that surgery to insert plastic tubes and/or remove adenoids is the best treatment.

THE EAR IN SUMMER

In the summertime, earaches usually have another cause. If your child has been swimming a lot, or has perhaps been swimming in some new place and a day or two later complains of pain, try a little test: Pull on his earlobe. (Do it gently!) If that causes the pain to increase, it could be that your child has a case of **swimmer's ear.** Swimmer's ear is a bacterial infection of the outer ear canal. The bacteria in the water gets trapped inside the ear, and causes a painful inflammation.

For this condition, there are a number of home remedies. Many drug stores sell non-antibiotic ear drops which can be used to irrigate the ear canal in the hopes that the offending bacteria will be flushed out. People also use peroxide for the same thing. If those fail, then your doctor will have to prescribe antibiotic ear drops to attack the infection directly.

Swimmer's ear may cut into kids' summertime activities. Children who are prone to these infections may even have to stop swimming temporarily. Still, there are some preventative measures you can try before banning your child from the diving board. Ear plugs may help keep the water out of the ear, especially if they are worn under a tight-fitting bathing cap. Some parents find that applying antibiotic eardrops before swimming helps cut down on infections. Other parents pour a little peroxide into the ear and hold it in place with a cotton ball for a few minutes before letting their child swim. The hope is that this creates an environment that bacteria will find hostile.

BEANS IN HIS EARS

Some kids it seems just can't resist poking things into their ears. I've seen aluminum foil and paper, pop beads and little pieces of plastic parts off toys. Often parents don't even know these things are in their child's ear until they work their way out by themselves. But sometimes the objects work their way further into the ear, and cause pain or irritation. Dried beans and dried peas can be a special problem, since they swell with fluid and become trapped deep within the ear. Once I even saw what I thought was an eardrum with a large hole in it until I look closely and saw the word "Lifesaver" written around the rim of that hole. An entire Lifesaver had become lodged right up against this child's eardrum.

The best medicine for this kind of problem is prevention. As soon as you can, teach your children to keep everything—even their fingers—out of their ears; once something is lodged inside the ear, it can be difficult and painful to remove. Parents shouldn't try it themselves, though, because of the possibility of shoving it further down the ear canal. In fact, the biggest danger with foreign bodies in the ear are the people who try to get them out and wind up damaging the inside of the ear.

If the child is old enough, and cooperative enough, a pediatrician might be able to reach the object using forceps. Sometimes it takes a team in the hospital to immobilize the child's head, and then probe.

RED EARS

Often parents think that if their child's ear is red it is infected. There are other things that should be considered, though. Frequently a fever will redden the ears. Red ears are also associated with allergies and hives. Check the other symptoms. Does the child have a rash on some other part of his body? Do you know if he is allergic to some specific foods. Has this ear redness come on without any other telltale signs of a cold or ear infection, such as fever, runny nose or listlessness? If so, you might suspect an allergic reaction.

YOUR CHILD UNDER SIX MONTHS

Generally parents don't suspect ear infections in babies under two months. So the infection is frequently found by the doctor, after the child has been brought in for some other complaint.

We sometimes hospitalize babies under two months for an ear infection that we might just let pass in an older sibling. That's because the risk of infection is so much greater in very young children with immature immune systems. In little babies, the chances of an infection working its way into the bloodstream—where it becomes a serious problem—is great enough that we don't like to take the chance.

So check with your pediatrician immediately for a feverish baby, especially one who is irritable. In these early months, we like to check out everything, even if it later turns out to be minor. It is impossible for a parent to diagnose an ear infection in an infant because the signs are similar for many different conditions. The baby will be feverish, irritable and fussy and may vomit. You as parents will just simply notice that your baby isn't functioning right. Since babies that young don't point to their ears the way older kids do, it will be difficult for you to tell without an examination whether your baby has an ear infection, a urinary tract infection or some other problem.

The solution is simple: When your young baby has a fever, call your doctor.

CHECKLIST

Ear-tugging, crying, fussiness, a slight fever, especially in a child who is just getting over a cold: Suspect an ear infection. Try the treatments suggested in the following section. If the child can be made comfortable, you can wait to call the doctor in the morning for an ear examination and possible antibiotic treatment.

Crying, ear-tugging, fever and severe pain that suddenly stops: Suspect a ruptured eardrum. Call your doctor.

Diarrhea, loss of appetite, congestion, fussiness: Consult the section on diarrhea and constipation for other possible causes. If no other cause seems likely, suspect an ear infection. Attempt treatment to ease discomfort, and consult with your doctor during office hours.

Ear discomfort, crying and fussiness, but no fever. possibly some signs of hearing loss, like sitting too close to the television or failing to respond to questions: Suspect serous otitis, a buildup of fluid behind the eardrum. Consult the pediatrician during office hours.

Ear pain without a cold in the summertime. pulling on the earlobe makes the pain worse: Suspect swimmer's ear. Consult your pediatrician during office hours for treatment. Consider preventative measures.

Red, warm outer ears: Suspect an allergy. Observe the child.

TREATMENT

The first goal of home treatment is to make the child comfortable. If his pain can be alleviated, then it is safe to wait until morning to consult your doctor. But even if you can reduce the pain, don't hesitate to call the doctor the next day during office hours. An untreated ear infection can linger without symptoms.

The first treatment I would suggest is acetaminophen, the drug found in common childhood preparations like Tylenol. Don't treat your child with aspirin, because of the possibility of Reye's Syndrome. Treat your child according to age and body weight as directed on the package. Give the acetaminophen about 45 minutes to take effect.

In the meantime, I often suggest a time-honored treatment: oil in the ear. Warm up a little vegetable oil or olive oil to body temperature, and put a couple of drops into the ear that hurts. Many parents who have tried this trick tell me that it really relieves the discomfort, often enough to hold the child over until the acetaminophen takes hold. (Some pediatricians don't recommend this treatment, so check with your doctor.)

There are also oil-based ear anesthetics that are available by prescription. Some parents say that they keep these ear drops around the house just in case, and that they do work well to relieve the pain. Auralgan is one commonly-prescribed brand that is available.

Sometimes kids with ear infections feel more comfortable sleeping in a semi-upright position because when they lie down, the pressure causes their ear to throb. Try building up a little nest of blankets and pillows to allow the child to sleep in a propped-up position.

Even with all these treatments, it could wind up being a long night for both parents and kids. That can be especially tough on a household that has a demanding day ahead. Still, it helps to remember that an ear infection really is a pretty painful ailment, even when it's being treated. I find that a sympathetic parent—even a sleepy one—goes a long way towards comforting a kid in the throes of this bewildering and uncomfortable ailment.

If the earache starts in the morning, or develops at school, I will arrange to see him in the afternoon for a more complete diagnosis.

When treating ear infections with antibiotics, we try to choose one that is inexpensive and tastes good enough that a fussy child will welcome it. The typical antibiotic that pediatricians will often try first is amoxicillin, which is a pink, fruit-flavored antibiotic in the penicillin family. For children who might be allergic to penicillin, there are other antibiotics, like Ceclor, in the cephalosporin family, and Septra, in the family of sulfa drugs.

There is a more potent line of antibiotics that we try to save for more resistent infections. Thus we sometimes will turn to a kind of amoxicillin called Augmentin, or the cephalosporins. We try to reserve those for more serious cases, because they can cost four to five times the amount of the ordinary antibiotics.

For children with frequent ear infections, we have found that many are able to take one dose of antibiotics a day without ill effect as a preventative measure.

ASK DR. JOHN

QUESTION: I have antibiotics left over from my child's last ear infection two months ago. It's midnight and he's crying, and I don't want to bother the doctor. Can I just use the antibiotics I have left over?

ANSWER: My answer would be an informal yes, if the antibiotic was prescribed for that child. Don't switch other kids' prescriptions, though, because there can be differences in medicine dosages in kids of different ages, weights and medical histories. Also, don't use medications that are more than a season old because it's difficult to determine their shelf life. But if your child gets the same thing again in January that he had in December, I would say by all means start the same treatment. I don't know of any situations where a dose or two of antibiotics will hurt a child. But call your doctor as soon as possible to check on the child's condition.

QUESTION: My child doesn't ever seem to have had an ear infection, but lately he seems to be sitting too close to the television set and ignoring what the teacher is saying.

ANSWER: This is a very common complaint. The trick is to evaluate the nature of the problem. If the child is having trouble hearing in two different places (that is, if both teachers and parents notice that the child seems to be straining to hear, or if the parents notice that their child is both not answering their calls readily and is also sitting too close to the television), then we will consider a hearing problem. A single problem of appearing not to hear—whether it is in school, or at home—is more likely to be behavioral. The child may not be answering your call because he doesn't want to for some reason, or is ignoring the teacher because of some school-related issue. Those problems need to be worked out separately.

But if the problem truly appears to be related to his hearing, then we will suggest a hearing test, which can be reliably administered to children as young as six months.

QUESTION: My child has been diagnosed with an ear infection, has taken antibiotics for two days now and seems to be feeling better. He wants to play with his best friend. Can I let him do that?

ANSWER: Sure. Ear infections aren't contagious. If he's feeling better and his temperature is normal, by all means let him play. Young children will let you know what they should be allowed to do. Children will just naturally take it easy on their own if they are really feeling miserable.

QUESTION: We have a non-refundable trip to Europe booked for tomorrow. My child has just begun screaming and crying and tugging on his ear. I am afraid he has an ear infection. What should we do? I would hate to lose this trip, but I don't want to hurt my child. Can he fly safely?

ANSWER: This is a tough problem. There are certainly some

doctors who will rule out flying in this situation altogether. I'm not one of them; I would advise caution and careful consideration of exactly what stage of the illness the child is in, coupled with what you know about how your child responds to illnesses and medications. In any case, the child should be seen as soon as possible and put on antibiotics. The big problem is that the pressure changes during take off and landing can increase the pressure in ears that are already infected. A ruptured eardrum caused just by that increased pressure would be rare, but you are running the risk of putting your child through some pretty severe discomfort. If you must fly, I would concentrate on his comfort. Give him Tylenol just before the flight, and make sure he drinks during take off and landing to help equalize the pressure in the middle ear.

QUESTION: My kid's eardrum did rupture. What are the long-term consequences of that?

ANSWER: In this day and age, ruptured eardrums usually heal with antibiotic treatment. You should stop by about a week later to have the progress of the healing checked.

QUESTION: My kid has been on antibiotics almost all winter for ear infections. Does that have any long-term consequences? Isn't that bad for a kid?

ANSWER: The major problem with antibiotics is the possibility that the child may develop an allergy to them. Contrary to popular opinion, though, antibiotics don't affect the immune system; they fight bacteria. Some people with chronic conditions like rheumatic fever take antibiotics their whole lives.

EYES

Parents are especially sensitive about problems with their children's eyes. Eyes, after all, are one of our major links to the outside world. Anything that threatens our eyes, and therefore our sight, is very frightening.

What's more, children's eye problems often present themselves in very frightening ways. The eyes turn red, they swell up, they drip gunk—enough sometimes to stick the eyelids together. Even worse, children will often act as if they are in great discomfort, rubbing their eyes and crying. It makes parents feel so helpless to see kids tormented by problems with their eyes, which after all seem to be such fragile, delicate organs.

Parents' fears are usually exacerbated by the things they have seen or heard about in other countries. Outside the United States, especially in subtropical areas, there are serious bacterial and parasitic illnesses that do cause blindness. Whenever parents notice problems with their child's eyes, there seems to be a subconscious association with these very serious conditions.

There are, in fact, very serious, sight-threatening conditions that require a doctor's immediate care. These, however, are the result of **injury** and not illness. Aside from injury, however, kids' eye problems are scarier to look at than they are serious. In the developed world, the diseases of the eye that children are subject to are more annoying than threatening. They do require treatment, but they shouldn't be cause for alarm.

Usually the first thing you will notice is that the whites of his eyes have turned red. By asking a series of questions about other symptoms, and about your child's recent activities, we can try to figure out what causes this redness, and what to do about it.

Ask yourself:

❖ Is the redness in one or both eyes?
❖ Is there any discharge?
❖ Are the eyes itchy?
❖ Does he have any cold or flu symptoms?
❖ What season is it?
❖ Is the air pollution index bad?
❖ Are there smokers in the house?
❖ Has he been swimming?
❖ Has he been petting any animals?
❖ Has he been reading a lot, especially in dim light?
❖ Does he seem to have trouble seeing?

We ask these questions to try to determine what the cause of the problem is. First we need to determine if the eye was damaged through accident or injury. Then we need to see if the problem was caused by a virus or a bacteria. The third possibility is that the eye problem has been caused by an allergy or contact with some substance. Because so many of the symptoms are the same with eye problems, finding the cause can often help us eliminate the problem or determine what the treatment should be.

The first thing to do is ask what happened. A child old enough to talk may tell you. If not, there may be other people—a babysitter, a friend, an older sibling, a bystander—who can. If they say there's been some accident like a poke with a stick, or a hit with a ball, then you'll know you're dealing with an eye injury.

You may not get a clear answer even though you suspect injury. One hint is to look carefully to see if the problem is present in one or both eyes. This will help us rule out accidents or injuries. If a kid has been poked with a stick, or hit by a baseball it's most likely the problem is affecting only the eye that has been struck or poked. So if both eyes are red, we can usually rule out accidents as a cause. (It doesn't necessarily work the other way around, though. If only one eye is red, it may still mean that a virus, bacteria or some other irritant is affecting only one eye.)

We'll discuss accidents or injuries at the end of this chapter. Skip immediately to the section on **eye injury** if you think something has happened to your child's eye.

But for the moment, let's presume that you have been able to pretty much rule out trauma, and are instead facing a kid with two red, gunky eyes.

RED EYES WITH DISCHARGE

One of the more common calls I get is from parents who call me, not with a problem, but with the diagnosis.

"Doctor, he's got **pinkeye**," the parents will say.

So what symptoms did they see that led them to this conclusion?

"The whites of his eye are inflamed. They're all red. When he woke up this morning there was sticky stuff all over the outside. His eye has been running thick, gooey stuff, and just now when he woke up from his nap, the sticky stuff was so thick that his eyes stuck shut."

Usually with those symptoms I will say, "Yes, you are right. He has pinkeye." But what is pinkeye? It is one of the most common and most misunderstood conditions of childhood. I find that parents are very frightened of pinkeye and the possible harm it may cause. What's more, they are often either embarrassed that their child has contracted it, or angry at the school or day-care center for "letting" their child get it. There is often an unspoken fear that pinkeye is somehow related to uncleanliness, or to bad parenting or sloppy hygeine at the day-care center. For working parents, too, there is the fear that the child won't be allowed back to school for a while. Actually, pinkeye isn't a very serious condition. And while it's contagious, it's no more so than a common cold. In fact, pinkeye *is* a cold in the eye.

The medical name for pinkeye is **conjunctivitis.** It is usually caused by the same virus that gives your child a runny nose and makes him sneeze. Indeed, the first symptom of a coming cold will often be the runny, sticky symptoms of pinkeye. I will tell parents to be aware that pinkeye sometimes means a cold is coming. Pinkeye also frequently accompanies sinusitis.

Kids' eyes may also be sensitive to light for a while.

Although the symptoms of pinkeye and colds are usually seen in the wintertime, there are summertime viruses that cause red, gooey eyes. Often you will also see the symptoms of summertime viruses like gastrointestinal problems and possibly rashes.

In the summertime, kids can pick up conjunctivitis while swimming, either from other people swimming in the same pool, or from bacteria that can be found in some lakes and ponds.

There are two types of conjunctivitis: bacterial and viral. But there is very little to tell bacterial and viral eye infections apart. That's why doctors will often prescribe an anti-bacterial eye drop or ointment as a precaution. In my experience, though, these eye drops are often useless because kids put up such a fuss that most of the drops or ointment don't get into the eye where they can do any good—and the infection clears up in a day or two anyway.

Some of the ointments most often prescribed have their own hazards. They come in tubes that are hard to use. A parent has to be extra careful applying cream from these tubes. It's all too easy to poke a squirmy baby or child in the eye with the tube. Because of this, some doctors will only use drops or may prescribe oral antibiotics if they feel that the infection is bacterial and it's going to be impossible to apply ointment to a particularly wiggly kid.

Besides these antibiotics, the best treatment is to gently daub the eye. Some old first-aid manuals recommend boric acid as an eye wash. That's fine, although I find that warm water works just as well. If the eyes are stuck together, it may take two people—if only because the child may tend to panic. Try to soothe the child, and stay calm yourself. Put the wet cotton ball or soft washcloth on the child's eyelid, and let it soften the crusted discharge until it can be wiped away without scratching. The child's eye will then open easily.

RED, ITCHY EYES

Allergic conjunctivitis is almost as common as conjunctivitis caused by bacteria or viruses. It will look pretty much the same too: red eyes with discharge. That means that it's pretty hard to tell them apart. One clue will be the itching. While bacterial or viral conjunctivitis is sometimes itchy, allergic conjunctivitis will almost always be.

You might also notice that your child is sneezing, or has a runny nose, but doesn't seem to have a fever or any other sign of a summertime cold.

Hard though it may be, one reason to try to figure out whether the conjunctivitis has an allergic cause, is so that whatever caused the problem can be avoided in the future. Most cases of allergic conjunctivitis will clear up quickly if the allergen is removed. Allergic reactions are somewhat more common in the warmer months than in the winter.

So ask yourself where your child has been and what he's been doing. Have you been out to the country recently? Picking wild flowers? Did he develop the same kind of red, itchy eyes last year at the same time? Have you been to a petting zoo, or over to see your friend with the cats? Pets are a common cause of allergic conjunctivitis. The child will pet an animal and then rub his eyes, carrying the allergen to the eyes.

If your child has a clear-cut reaction to a flower or a weed or a particular pet, your only solution is to keep him away from it. Unfortunately that may mean banning romps with Fluffy.

Eye allergies aren't threatening, but they can be extremely uncomfortable. Our treatment, until the allergic reaction subsides, consists mainly of making the child comfortable. Decongestant eye drops like Visine can help ease the itching and redness. Steroid drops are also sometimes prescribed.

RED EYES—NO ITCHING, NO DISCHARGE

What if your child's eyes are red and are bothering him, but there is no discharge? Red swollen eyes can be caused by **irritation.**

Summertime is definitely a season for irritation. Often you will notice the cause right away. He will come out of the swimming pool with bright red eyes, and you will realize immediately that he's had too much **exposure to chlorine.** The solution is easy: Everybody get out of the pool! While your child's eyes may burn and feel uncomfortable for a while, this irritation isn't a major problem and will clear up on its own if left alone. Swimming goggles may also help.

Kids' eyes can also become irritated from **air pollution.** If you live in an area where air pollution is a problem, you will hear on the radio that the pollution index is high. Don't be fooled if you yourself aren't bothered. No two people respond to irritants exactly the same way. You can keep kids indoors on days when the smog and pollutants are bad. Air conditioning can also be a big help.

One thing you can do something about is eye irritation caused by **smoking.** Aside from the tremendous respiratory problems I see in kids who grow up in households with smokers, I also often see kids whose eyes itch and burn for no other reason than that Mom and Dad smoke. The solution is simple, and you know what it is.

EYE PAIN WITH NO OTHER SYMPTOMS

What if your child complains that his eyes hurt, but you notice no redness or other eye symptoms? Look closely. You may notice other symptoms like runny nose, or congestion or a cough, especially at night.

If so, you might consider **sinusitis.** The sinuses are located right behind the eyes. Sinusitis usually begins with a cold or an allergy. The mucus gets trapped in the sinuses, providing a breeding ground for bacteria. Head or eye pain frequently result.

A sinus infection should be seen by a doctor who may prescribe antibiotics. You can also in the meantime use acetaminophen to relieve the pain.

Sometimes other illnesses will first be apparent through a pain in the eyes. A child coming down with **infectious mononucleosis** may first complain of painful eyes, as will a child in the early stages of **flu.** Your course in this case is to check for other symptoms and if you find none, wait and check again.

You might also suspect **eyestrain** if your child complains of painful eyes. Don't be surprised, though, if eye pain or headache is the only symptom. It's a common misconception that eyestrain leads to eye redness. Think back and try to remember if your child has been reading in too little light, reading too much or playing Nintendo for too long. Another possibility is that your child's vision needs correcting.

EYE RUBBING

"There's something in my eye!"

Until this point, all the conditions we have discussed usually involve redness or discomfort in both eyes. Viruses, bacteria, allergies, flu or eyestrain all usually affect both eyes equally. Conjunctivitis can start in one eye. But to be safe, if your child complains of pain in only one eye, or comes to you with redness in only one eye, we start thinking of other causes immediately.

One of the most common causes of eye discomfort is **dust or dirt** blown in the eye. Even insects can fly into eyes, and become trapped in the folds of the lid. Usually these problems can be handled at home by flushing the eye with water. Once the flecks or foreign bodies are removed, and the eye is flushed out with water or a mild eyewash solution, the eye should return to looking and feeling normal in a few hours.

If it doesn't, and the eye remains red and painful, your child should be seen by a doctor. It is possible that whatever was in his eye has caused a **corneal abrasion.** A corneal abrasion isn't as bad as it sounds. In fact, I believe most corneal abrasions go untreated because there isn't much in the way of symptoms. All it means is that the cornea—the transparent covering right over the pupil—has been scratched. A kid with a mild corneal abrasion will continue to feel that there is something in his eye after you have flushed the actual speck out. He may continue to rub his eye and complain. That's because the scratch does burn and does feel irritated, just as if the dirt fleck or grain were actually still there.

The doctor will be able to check your child's eye for a foreign body or a corneal abrasion.

Abrasions aren't usually that serious. Still, I recommend that you call your doctor, who will then decide whether the eye needs to be examined by an ophthalmologist. While the condition can most likely be treated with eye drops, it still is a good idea to have scratches checked, just in case they're more serious than they appear. There might be a foreign body still lodged in the eye or a scratch that is deeper than expected.

What's more, a doctor may prescribe a patch to be worn over the sore eye to prevent rubbing and scratching. Scratches that aren't in themselves problems should still be seen by a doctor because there is a possibility that they might become infected. So an ophthalmologist may want to prescribe antibiotic drops to prevent infection.

EYE INJURIES

When an eye is injured, often you will know that something has happened, either you were there and watched it, or your child or someone else reports it to you. Even if no one tells you, however, a single red or painful eye and a crying child are clues enough to begin thinking "injury." Even if you think it's nothing more than a bump or a fleck of dirt in the eye, watch your child closely and ask yourself these questions:

❖ Is the problem in one eye only?

❖ Did it come on suddenly?

❖ Can your child or any other child remember anything happening?

❖ Is your child holding his eye?

❖ Is the child complaining of pain, or saying that he can't see?

What are some typical cases that I see? A child will come in from the playground crying. He's been hit in the eye by another kid, who had been flailing his arms about while playing. An older child will come off the soccer field holding his eye. He's been hit by a soccer ball and won't open his eye. A baby begins to cry in the other room, and clutches his fist to his eye. Meanwhile, his five-year-old brother shrinks into the corner looking sheepish, and will later be coaxed into admitting that he accidentally jabbed his X-Man into his baby brother's eye.

The key behavior you will notice in the case of injury is that the child will hold his eye. With dust or dirt in the eye, your child will be rubbing his eye and complaining.

If there has been a serious injury, on the other hand, the child will typically refuse to open his eye at all. He may complain of pain. He may say he can't see. He may even refuse altogether to take his hand away from his eye. It may be very difficult for you to get a look at the eye at all. My advice to parents: Take this behavior seriously. If he won't let you look at his eye at all, don't force his hand away from his eye. Call your doctor instead, or get him to an emergency room. Chances are high that something has happened that requires a doctor's immediate care.

The range of possible eye injuries are too complex and too medically detailed to go into here. Most of them, even ones as serious as bleeding in the eyeball, can be successfully treated in the emergency room, or with a brief hospital stay.

YOUR CHILD UNDER SIX MONTHS

I often get calls from parents of newborns who see **lint** floating on the surface of their baby's eye. They want to know if they should try to take it off. The answer is no. Babies may get lint in their eyes because they are so often wrapped or dressed in soft fuzzy things. Leave it alone and tears in the eye itself will take care of it.

Newborns also often awaken, as do their older brothers and sisters, with their eyes stuck together with a gooey, or dried crusty substance. It can look scary, especially if your teeny baby can't open his eyes. In fact, it isn't usually a serious condition. In most cases, it's caused by a **narrowed tear duct.**

In many newborn babies, the tear duct is still a little too narrow at first to let nighttime tears drain out as they are supposed to. Instead, they dry in the eyes. This condition is common in babies in the first weeks of life, and continues to be very common for about a month or two. It can persist as long as six months.

This condition is so common that the pediatrician visiting the child in the hospital usually tells parents to expect it. The most common treatment is the same as that for conjunctivitis: daub the child's eyes with cotton balls soaked in warm water. The point is simply to remove the crust so the child can open his eyes. If there is redness or swelling, check with the doctor for possible infection.

Usually, the child grows out of this condition without any further difficulty. If, however, the symptoms persist past six months, we usually recommend that the child see an ophthalmologist. That's because the tear duct may have remained closed and may need opening up surgically.

CHECKLIST

ONE RED EYE: Consider eye injury. Consult your doctor immediately.

EYE PAIN WITH REDNESS: Consider eye injury. Consult your doctor immediately.

EYE RUBBING: Consider dust or dirt in the eye, or a scratch on the eye. Flush with water. If scratchy feeling persists, consult your doctor.

EYE CLUTCHING: Consider eye injury. Consult your doctor immediately.

RED EYES WITH DISCHARGE: Consider conjunctivitis. If desired, or required by the school, consult your doctor for eye drops or other medication.

RED EYES WITH RUNNY NOSE OR PROLONGED COUGH: Consider sinusitis. Treat with acetaminophen for discomfort. Consult your doctor if it persists.

RED, ITCHY EYES: Consider allergic conjunctivitis. If desired or required by the school, consult your doctor for eye drops or other medication.

RED EYES—NO ITCHING, NO DISCHARGE: Consider irritation from air pollution, chlorine or cigarette smoke.

SHALL I WAKE THE DOCTOR?

Eye injuries are the only conditions that warrant a midnight call to the doctor, who may decide to meet you in the emergency room. All the other conditions of the eye can safely wait until morning for discussion and treatment.

CAN HE GO BACK TO SCHOOL?

Because they fear the kind of criticism I discussed earlier, most schools and day-care centers won't let a child with pinkeye back until some treatment has begun. In actuality, though, if your school has no such prohibition, there's no need to keep her home if she isn't uncomfortable. Schools usually permit attendance once antibiotic drops are started. Pinkeye is contagious, but it is no more contagious, and no more harmful, than the common cold. And we can't keep kids out of school for every cold!

Whether or not you keep a child home for any of the other eye conditions also depends on her comfort.

With eye injuries, however, you should consult the ophthalmologist, since some eye injuries are serious enough that the doctor may wish to restrict the child's movements for a while.

ASK DR. JOHN

QUESTION: Does conjunctivitis cause blindness?

ANSWER: No. The only major causes of blindness in the United States are premature birth and injury. A hit in the eye with a hardball, a poke with a toy arrow, damage to the eye in an auto accident all might cause blindness in the affected eye. But there aren't any illnesses that pose that threat.

QUESTION: A number of kids in the neighborhood have gotten pinkeye after swimming in the municipal pool. Should we stop swimming there for the summer?

ANSWER: If you like. But it would be sort of like not going to basketball games because your kids got colds there. Pinkeye—or conjunctivitis—is a cold in the eye and is as contagious as any other cold. If a virus that causes conjunctivitis is going around the kids who swim in the municipal pool, chances are that your child will develop a resistance after one exposure, and won't catch it a second time. Of course, while he has the conjunctivitis, you might keep him out of the swimming pool so that the chlorine won't irritate his eyes.

LUMPS, BUMPS
AND BRUISES

Whenever a parent calling about a lump on a child's body begins, "Doctor, I need to see you right away," I know the parent on
the other end of the line isn't thinking about swollen glands. She
isn't thinking about bug bites or cat scratches. She isn't even thinking about conditions like mononucleosis or strep throat. No, the
worried parents have something even more serious on their minds.
They are thinking about cancer.

It's a natural fear. Nearly every adult knows someone who has
discovered a lump—in a breast, or other body part—that has turned
out to be cancer. What's more, many of the leading family-oriented
magazines seem to devote large portions of one issue or another to
stories of kids who either did or didn't recover from cancer. This
makes it seem as if cancer is a much more frequent occurrence than
it actually is.

Because so many parents equate lumps with cancer, in each
section as we go along below, I will tell you how we look for cancer,
and how these symptoms differ from the ordinary symptoms most
parents see.

Remember: We are rarely considering cancer. In fact,
cancer in children is quite uncommon, much rarer than cancer in

adults. In the average practice doctors see thousands of cases of swollen glands from a virus for every case of childhood cancer.

Don't get me wrong: We should always be alert to the more serious possibilities. Many times I will ask to see a child who I am virtually certain has a viral infection. I'll see her for my own and her parents' peace of mind. I want to rule out that tiny chance. But we need to keep our worries in perspective: We are examining the child as a *precaution,* and not because we expect to discover cancer.

When we evaluate a lump, we ask ourselves a number of questions about the lump itself, and about what the child has been doing in the immediate past:

- ❖ Where is the lump?
    - On the neck?
    - In the groin?
    - Under the skin?
    - On the surface of the skin?
    - On an arm or a leg?
    - Under the arms?
    - At the base of the skull?
- ❖ Does the child have a fever?
- ❖ Has she been bitten by an insect?
- ❖ Scratched by an animal?
- ❖ Has she fallen or been struck by something?

Usually lumps are associated with some other condition. By asking these questions we can try to narrow down the possible causes.

LUMPS UNDER THE SKIN

Nearly every parent at one time or another has come across one: a lump, pea-sized or even larger, under the skin especially in the neck or head area. The most likely cause is **swollen glands,** which are associated with a number of different conditions. Among other things, swollen glands can be caused by **viral infections,**

bacterial infections, insect bites, animal scratches, strep throat, ear infections, impetigo, or **mononucleosis.**

Why do kids' glands swell up so easily, when adults glands do not? It's actually part of their defense against illness. Infants and children have what we call reactive lymph tissue. That means their lymph glands react easily to infection.

Although the phenomenon is normal, it can be frightening, because it means that kids' glands can very quickly swell up to quite an enormous size. Glands that swell to the size of a walnut aren't uncommon.

Where do you find swollen glands? Nearly anyplace on the body. The glands we are talking about are lymph nodes which are part of the body's defense system against infections. The map of the lymph system looks like a map of the interstate highway system. There are lymph glands all over the body, any of which can become swollen. Many of these glands may swell in different places for different reasons, and may look slightly different as well.

We'll consider swollen glands by the places they occur, and by their possible causes. The head and neck area are the most common places to find swollen glands. That's because so many of the possible causes of swollen glands originate in this area. You can find large swollen glands at the base of the skull, or under the jaw just under and forward of the ears, along the side of the neck itself or under the chin.

One possible cause is simply a **viral infection.** The same viral infection that can cause runny noses, sore throats, sneezing, runny eyes and coughs can also cause glands to swell up. The key is how the child is feeling and behaving otherwise. If the child has had a cold or a fever and slightly swollen glands for two to three days, but appears to be getting better, then we aren't too concerned about the swelling.

If, however, the fever and cold symptoms don't seem to be getting any better, and the gland remains swollen, then the child should be examined by a doctor. It's possible that antibiotic treatment is needed. What are the possibilities?

Strep throat can cause swollen glands. Strep throat—a bacterial infection of the throat—needs to be treated with antibiotics. So if your child is running a fever, and complaining about a sore throat along with the swollen glands, consult your physician. Read the sore throat section of the chapter on pain for more information.

The lymph glands can also become infected themselves with bacteria, usually staphylococcus. That usually happens when bacteria enter the child's system through an animal scratch or a bug bite. This condition is called **lymphadenitis.** It can cause truly spectacular swelling. This kind of swollen gland is different from others. The glands are not only large, but they are hard and hot to the touch, the skin around them is red, and the child usually will have a fever.

I know that we are dealing with a case of lymphadenitis which does require a doctor's care and treatment, when I get the phone call from parents. "Doctor," they say, "I've seen swollen glands before, but never like these. These are so hot I can barely touch them."

Ear infections can also be associated with swollen glands. Read the chapter on ears for more information about ear infections.

What if your child has been feverish and ill for a week or so and suddenly gets swollen glands? Then there's a possibility that your child has **mononucleosis.** With mononucleosis, your child can seem pretty sick. Her behavior—one of the clues we look closely at—will change tremendously. She may be lethargic, and whiny, and cry over things that normally don't bother her. (The swollen glands from mononucleosis can appear in the neck, but they can also appear anywhere else on the body, and may in fact be found in several places.) If you suspect mononucleosis, check with your doctor. We do a blood test to confirm the diagnosis.

Mononucleosis symptoms can cause a lot of fear in parents. That's because parents fear that the symptoms indicate, not something less serious, but something more serious, like **leukemia.** Leukemia symptoms are in fact a lot like those of mononucleosis. While it is true that kids do get leukemia, it's just that mono is so much more common, and leukemia so much more rare.

Infection with the virus that causes mononucleosis, is nearly universal. It's rare to find an adult who has not had it. It's a less severe disease in younger children than in adolescents and young adults, and often resembles the flu.

When they are bathing their children, parents can often find lumps in the groin. These may be caused by a virus, but are frequently caused by **infected scratches** or **insect bites.**

Scratches and bites can also cause glands in the neck and head to swell. That's because the glands nearest to the scratch that tend to swell up as the body marshals its defenses to fight the infection. I have found that swollen glands I couldn't explain were sometimes caused by scratches in the scalp; I had to do quite some prowling through the hair before I finally hit on the cause.

The skin infection known as **impetigo** can also cause swollen glands in the area near the skin rash. (See the section on rashes for more information about impetigo.)

A skin infection that leads to swollen glands should be seen by a doctor. We handle these kinds of swollen glands by treating the underlying infection. We treat the infected scratch with an antibiotic ointment like Bacitracin, watch the gland and see if the swelling goes down. If the swelling doesn't go down, we may need to turn to an oral antibiotic.

LUMPS ON THE SKIN

Probably most parents easily recognize the most common cause of lumps on the skin: **insect bites.** I often get calls from parents worried because insect bites have blown up into large lumps. I tell them not to worry. It's just a local reaction. Insect bites can swell quite dramatically, especially on the face and hands. The serious kinds of allergic reactions to bee stings—known as anaphylaxis—happen very quickly after the sting itself, long before and unrelated to the size of the lump. Anaphylaxis causes weakness, breathing trouble, and sometimes loss of consciousness.

Another common cause of lumps on the skin is **warts.** Despite the folklore that warts are caused by touching frogs and toads, it is just that—folklore. What many people don't know is that warts are caused by a virus.

The first thing you'll probably notice is a hard, painless lump which expands. Warts can be found on just about any part of the body, although not generally on the face. We often find them on the extremities. Kids' little fingers get warts. There are also warts that are found on the flat surface of the feet that are called plantar warts, because that's the name of the surface itself.

One thing we can do about warts is to simply leave them alone. If they aren't painful, that's the best approach. Sooner or later (and later may be a long time—a year or more) they'll just go away by themselves. However, warts on the soles of the feet can be painful because pressure on the wart causes discomfort when the child is walking. In those circumstances, use over-the-counter preparations with mild acids are available to shrink the wart.

For more serious warts, or a more thorough job, a dermatologist should be consulted. One thing you should not do, however, is attempt to shave the wart away or to cut it out. Not only will it hurt the child, but it can become infected.

LUMPS ON THE HEAD

One of the most frequent causes of bumps on the head is also the simplest: **falling.** She falls backwards out of a tree, bangs her head and pow! Up comes a big goose egg.

Hard blows to the head are potentially serious, and usually do merit at least a call to your doctor to check. But if she is otherwise all right, seems to recover rapidly from the trauma of the fall, isn't vomiting, losing consciousness, or complaining of dizziness or severe headache, then I wouldn't be too concerned about the lump. The size of the lump on the outside isn't an indication that something bad has happened in the brain.

Apply ice packs to reduce the swelling, as long as your child doesn't find the ice more objectionable than the lump itself. (Those blue picnic cooler packs sometimes work better than ice; I know some parents keep one in the freezer just in case.) With or without ice, the swelling should subside within a day or two. If it doesn't, check with your doctor.

Another cause for lumps on the head is the same as for lumps under the skin: **swollen lymph glands.** The lymph glands at the nape of the neck can swell just as other lymph glands can. Lumps in that position, stuck between the bone and the skin with no fat in between, can look large. These lumps aren't associated with any trauma like falling, or being whacked by a flying toy. They are freely movable under the skin.

Swelling on the head in places where there are no lymph glands—like on the top of the head—is unusual when there hasn't been any trauma. But occasionally we will find **dermoid cysts.** Those are remnants of embryonic tissue that can swell up into cysts. They are usually found at the midline of the head (the place where your child's hair would be if she had a Mohawk cut). Although they are uncommon, they are usually found in younger children. This needs a call to the doctor.

LUMPS ON THE ARMS AND LEGS

Falling, banging and **bruising** are also the leading causes of lumps on the arms and legs. The same kind of swelling that occurs on the skull can also occur any place the skin has been smacked. As with these kinds of lumps on the head, they aren't serious, and should subside within a day or two. They don't require any special treatment, although ice can be helpful in reducing the swelling.

Sometimes parents will notice lumps along the shin on both legs that are tender and swollen. These lumps can be a yellow or greenish shade and about the size of a nickel. These lumps are fairly common and are frequently found in kids who have other symptoms like fever or strep throat. This is called **erythema nodosum.** It can indicate a sensitivity to medication. I find that these lumps are more common in slightly older kids than in younger ones, and more common in girls than in boys.

Parents often worry about lumps that seem to be on their kids' bones. They worry that the lump might be a tumor. Tumors, like other kinds of cancer, are rare in kids. But parents are right to be concerned. If there is no ready explanation for them, something that feels like a bone lump in kids should be looked at by a doctor.

When we spot a lump on a shin or an arm for example, the first thing we will do is to ask the kid what happened. If you saw a collision, or if we hear from the child herself or from friends or her babysitter that there was a bang, then we relax a bit and wait for the bump to go down. One way to tell if the lump on the bone is something to take seriously is whether or not it can be moved. A lump that can move under the skin is probably okay. A lump that is fixed—as if it is a part of the bone—needs to be checked by a doctor.

If there is a lump that doesn't move and there was no bang or bump that you know of, the doctor may send your child off for an x-ray. That's because there is in fact a remote possibility that a bone lump is a **tumor.** Just to put things in perspective, though: We order x-rays mainly as precautions.

One exception to our concerns about lumps on the bones is a lump right where the ribs join in the front. Often children will develop small lumps—the size of a pea—right on that bone. This is normal.

THE LUMPS AREN'T MUMPS

Most parents still expect that the swelling under their child's jaw might be caused by **mumps.** That's because they themselves probably had an uncomfortable bout with mumps, which is a viral illness that causes a swelling of the salivary glands.

The fact is, your kids won't get mumps the way you did. The measles-mumps-rubella vaccine that all kids now get has pretty much eliminated mumps.

It's a good thing too. Mumps weren't just an inconvenience. They also had some potentially serious side effects, including hearing loss and the possibility of sterility.

YOUR CHILD UNDER SIX MONTHS

Everything that causes a lump in an older child also causes lumps in babies. Embryonic cysts are slightly more common in babies than in older children.

A swelling in a baby's groin or scrotum could indicate an **inguinal hernia.** This kind of swelling is soft and squishy to the touch. It is usually small, although it can sometimes be as large as a walnut. Although these hernias appear alarming—and do require surgery—they are completely repairable. If this kind of swelling is accompanied by prolonged crying, however, you should call the doctor immediately because it could indicate an **incarcerated hernia,** a condition that requires quick treatment.

Swelling in a baby's scrotum might also be caused by a **hydrocele.** That is a fluid collection in the scrotum that doesn't usually need to be treated unless it is also associated with a hernia.

Umbilical hernias cause swelling at the belly button. We don't usually treat those either. If left alone, they will generally disappear with time.

CHECKLIST

LUMPS UNDER THE SKIN: Consider swollen glands, which are associated with a number of different conditions. Swollen glands can be caused by viral infections, insect bites, animal scratches, strep throat, ear infections, impetigo, or mononucleosis.

LUMPS ON THE SKIN: With red swollen lumps, consider insect bites. With rough, hard, pea-sized lumps, consider warts.

LUMPS ON THE HEAD: After a fall or hit, consider trauma. At nape of neck, consider swollen glands. On top of head, consider embryonic cysts.

LUMPS ON THE ARMS AND LEGS: After fall or hit, consider trauma. Immovable lump with no trauma associated, consider tumor.

SHALL I WAKE THE DOCTOR?

Most lumps don't require a doctor's immediate attention. Even if you discover a lump that you fear might be cancer, an evaluation can wait until morning. A 12-hour wait would have no effect on the course of the disease.

Head lumps caused by mild trauma don't require immediate medical attention unless they are accompanied by other symptoms like vomiting, dizziness or loss of consciousness.

The one lump I wouldn't mind being awakened to discuss is that associated with **lymphadenitis.** That means the gland is not only swollen but hot to the touch and is accompanied by a fever. With such an infection I might want to send the child to the emergency room even in the middle of the night for an examination, and possible antibiotic therapy.

CAN SHE GO BACK TO SCHOOL?

It isn't usually necessary to stay home from school because of lumps.

If the lumps are swollen glands associated with a strep throat, the child should stay at home until antibiotic treatment causes the fever to subside and she begins to feel better. Generally her behavior will help you determine when she is feeling ready to go back to school. Her contagious period ends once treatment is begun.

In young children, mononucleosis doesn't usually signal a long period of convalescence the way it does with older kids. While in adolescence it can cause a lengthy period of tiredness and just plain feeling crummy, a younger child with mono will often be more or less like a kid with the flu. Again, the child's behavior will govern when she goes back to school.

ASK DR. JOHN

QUESTION: I'm worried about this new super-bacteria I've read about—the one that can be fatal. Doesn't it start in bruises?

ANSWER: First off, let me stress that this virulent strain of streptococcal bacteria may have been around for a long time. As far as anyone knows, the incidence is not rising. There are a few fatalities from it every year, but these cases are very rare and unpredictable. Often they appear to start as an ordinary case of strep throat. Sometimes, though, the entry point of the bacteria will be a cut or a bruise. To be safe, observe bruises and cuts. While bruises may become much more spectacularly colored as time goes on—changing from blush red to purple to gold—the pain should decrease, never increase. If the pain of a bruise or cut becomes more intense, or if the bruise becomes hot to the touch, seek medical attention immediately, as a course of antibiotics may be required.

NOSES

Before anyone decides to become a pediatrician, he or she should sit at the end of my telephone line on some late February afternoon and listen to parents describe their kids' runny noses.

"It's green, doctor," they say. "It started out clear, but then it got yellowish, and now it's all green and sticky. . . ."

And on and on it goes, all afternoon.

A cold is not a serious illness. But it is probably the single most common illness that humankind suffers. Colds are the single exception to the general observation that kids on balance are healthier than adults. Kids, because they are new to this world, get far more colds than adults do. And colds mean runny noses.

Runny noses are also an exception to my general rule that what parents most often need from me is reassurance that their child's symptoms aren't signs of some serious, life-threatening ailment. In my experience, parents aren't usually worried about their kids' runny noses. If anything, they find them kind of annoying. Who can blame them? Runny noses *are* annoying, and definitely more for adults than for the kids who have them. In fact, it's the kids' blissful ability to ignore noses that are running down to their shoelaces that so irritates adults. Runny noses mean more work for teachers who must hand out or wield Kleenex all day. It can mean days off from school for a child who isn't really very sick, just socially unacceptable. It's also a condition that can make your adorable little moppet grossly unappealing. Just remember how you felt the last time you saw one of your friends' runny-nosed kids wandering among the hors d'oeuvres, and you'll get the general idea.

That said, there is one condition a runny nose can signal that is more serious than just the run-of-the-mill cold. Runny noses, if they go on long enough, can be signs of **sinusitis.** While sinusitis isn't serious in and of itself, it does require treatment. As with the other conditions we describe in this book, it is the behavior and symptoms associated with the runny nose itself that will give us the clues we need to evaluate your child's condition.

WHAT ARE RUNNY NOSES AND HOW DO KIDS GET THEM?

A runny nose is the most obvious side effect of a cold. Colds are caused by a cold virus, which means the cold and the runny nose are easy to transmit, and nearly impossible to "cure."

Why do noses run? Nasal tissue normally produces mucus, which acts like a filter, trapping particles before they get into the lungs. Viral infections cause the tissue to become inflamed and irritated. Inflamed nasal tissue produces lots of mucus, which has no place to go but out.

How do we get colds? From other people. The weather itself also has something to do with it. For a long time we thought it was an old wives' tale that cold weather brought colds, and that by bundling up we could help prevent colds. New research is showing, however, that grandmother was right. If you don't wear your galoshes or dress warmly you may very well get a cold. We don't know yet whether the cold virus incubates more efficiently when the weather is colder, or whether it is simply that when a body is fighting to warm itself up in the cold weather, it is more vulnerable to attack by a cold virus. Either way, the message is the same: Make him wear a hat. Make him change his wet socks. Make him wear his galoshes. Modern-day research can't tell us everything, so while it may not help, it couldn't hurt.

Nonetheless, you will find that despite your best efforts your child will get not one cold but several every winter. Your child will probably get more colds than you do. Your child may pass almost seamlessly from one cold to another. It may seem that it has been months since you have last been able to leave the house without a big wad of tissues in your pocket.

The fact is, kids do get lots of colds. That's because they're pretty new to this world and haven't yet built up resistances to all the different varieties of cold germs there are out there. So colds that might pass you or me by will stick with your toddler and give him a runny nose. It isn't unusual for kids to get six to eight colds a winter. Think about it: That's two or three colds a month. So, since colds typically last for nearly a week, it isn't at all unusual for a child to have a runny nose for two or three weeks out of every winter month. No wonder parents think their kids are constantly sick. They are!

HOW DO WE KNOW IF IT'S SERIOUS?

A typical cold that leads to a runny nose will begin with a fever. Not a high fever, necessarily, but a temperature high enough to make your child lethargic and cranky. (The exact range of temperature will vary from child to child. Read the chapter about fever for more information.) Your child may have runny eyes and may sneeze a lot. He may complain of stuffiness and of a headache. Then as the mucus drains the runny nose begins. You may notice a cough beginning at the same time as the mucus draining down the back of the throat triggers a cough.

At some point during the course of this cold, your child may feel sick enough to stay out of school or day-care. But in my experience, kids bounce right back from these colds and don't require any special care.

As I said earlier, some day-care centers may want the child to stay home for a while, but in my experience, that's largely because the center fears criticism, and not out of actual concern for the child. If your child is old enough, a little training may help: Cover your mouth when you cough. (We now recommend teaching a child to cough into his elbow, not his palm. It turns out germs are largely spread by hand-to-hand contact, and not through the air.) Use your handkerchief, not your sleeve.

Parents usually can tolerate colds up to a point. It is when the nasal discharge begins to change color that they worry. I find that parents become concerned when the runny part of the runny nose changes from clear or milky-colored to yellow or green.

There is some disagreement nowadays, even among doctors, as to the significance of that color change. It used to be widely accepted that a change to a green or yellowish discharge meant that the infection had changed from viral to bacterial. That still may be true. Now, however, we tend to look more at the length of time a single episode has gone on, and at whether a child who has seemed to be getting better begins to get worse again or starts running a fever.

Because kids do go from cold to cold all winter, it can sometimes be difficult to determine just how long a single episode has gone on. We generally figure that if a child has had an uninterrupted runny nose for two or three weeks, that it's time to check to see if he has **sinusitis** no matter what the color of the discharge.

Sinusitis is an infection of the sinuses. It occurs when the bacteria that are normally present in everyone's system are able to infect the sinuses. That usually happens in conjunction with a cold and runny nose, since the stuffed-up sinuses and irritated mucus linings that the child already has from the cold provide a perfect breeding ground for bacteria.

Sinusitis almost never comes first. It almost always follows a cold. Young children are especially susceptible because their sinus drainage isn't very good in the first place.

One sign of sinusitis is coughing at night. If it goes on for longer than a week, or becomes harsher and more raspy, it could be a sign that the sinuses are draining infected material and that the child should be examined.

In any case, a child with sinusitis begins to look sicker than a child who just has an endless series of colds. The child may begin to develop circles under his eyes. He may be fussy and lose his appetite. Older kids may complain of headaches from the sinus pressure. They may also complain of a sore throat; that's from the scratchiness of coughing up the mucus that is draining down the back of the throat.

Sinusitis has always been a common diagnosis in adults. It was less commonly used for children, and is only recently becoming more recognized. A recently developed range of antibiotics also are quite effective against childrens' sinus infections.

ALLERGIES

What about kids who seem to have constant colds, who are always sneezing or who always seem to be rubbing their noses on their sleeves? We know that young kids get a lot of colds all year, but what if those colds never seem to take a break, and are never associated with fevers? What if those colds seem to come more in the spring and the summer, rather than in the winter when most everyone else is suffering?

It could be that your child doesn't have a cold at all, but rather an **allergy.**

I see such problems all the time. Sometimes it starts in the spring when the flowers begin to bud. Sometimes it's the late summer with pollens and ragweed. But sometimes there are other, more personal causes. The first trip to open up the vacation house can bring on an attack when the molds of the winter are disturbed. Sometimes, sadly, it starts when a family gets a pet. Pets are notorious causes of allergies: The child breathes in the pet's dander, or gets it on his hands or hair, and it sets up a reaction that includes sneezing, itching and runny eyes.

What is an allergy? It is a sensitivity to a particular substance that sets off a reaction in the body including itching and mucus production. Although we will sometimes eliminate milk or wheat from the child's diet for a while just to make sure, nasal allergies are most often caused by things that are inhaled.

The best treatment is to identify and remove the offending allergen. That usually means getting rid of the pet. I've seen many an otherwise happy relationship with a dog or a cat end because the child was allergic. If the child is allergic to the bunny, one of them is going to have to go. If the beach house causes problems, wait until after it's been aired out to bring him along.

Pollens and other outdoor allergens can't be helped. During the peak allergy season, allergies can be treated with an antihistamine like Benadryl. In severe cases, air conditioning the house may help. As a last resort, a trip to the allergist may be necessary for diagnosis and appropriate management.

Generally allergies are more annoying than serious. The most serious possible complication of nasal allergies is **sinus infection** which can develop as bacteria take advantage of the irritated nasal tissues.

NOSEBLEEDS

Nosebleeds occur fairly commonly in kids. That's because of two things: kids' habits and the structure of the inside of the nose. The blood vessels inside the nose are very close to the surface, and there are lots of them. And kids pick their noses. A little miscalculation on the child's part, and you can get an astonishing amount of blood from one very small nose.

What's more, once they begin, nosebleeds can recur quite often. That's because the original cut, when healing, forms a small scab which irritates the inside of the child's nose. Then he picks it off, which starts the bleeding all over again. It won't be unusual for a child who has one nosebleed to have two or three more over several days.

The general treatment for a nosebleed is simply to stop the bleeding. Sit the child upright and make him lean slightly forward. Then, with your forefinger and thumb acting like a clothespin, pinch the nose together and hold it for 15 minutes. The trickiest part of this, of course, is getting the child to cooperate. Read to him, put on cartoons, promise him a popsicle at the end—anything that will work—because at the end of that 15 minutes, the nosebleed will most likely be over.

If the first 15-minute period of pinching doesn't stop the bleeding, I usually recommend a second round. If that second effort doesn't work, then I suggest calling the physician or heading for the emergency room because there are occasional nosebleeds that won't stop. They require packing. The doctor or the emergency room staff will pack the nose with a special gauze to help stop the bleeding. In extreme cases, the portion of the nose that is bleeding may require cauterization.

If you know that your child is subject to nosebleeds or doesn't respond to the pinching method or has already had a nosebleed or two earlier in the same day, I would consult with your doctor right away. That's because occasionally—but rarely—a child with recurrent nosebleeds can lose enough blood that he needs to be treated separately for the blood loss.

For some reason, toddlers and young children love to experiment with their noses by shoving things up them. Only a mindreader would know why. But almost everything that can fit up a nose has reportedly been found there. My personal favorites are dried beans and peas that swell up with the mucus and become a challenge to remove. In addition, other common objects are: aluminum foil, pieces of tissue paper, and small parts of toys. Some of these objects can be lodged quite far up the nose and be impossible for a parent to remove. I have occasionally had to send a child to an ear-nose-throat specialist to remove a challenging object.

The condition isn't serious, but if the object remains stuck long enough, the child may develop a foul-smelling odor, because of the mucus trapped behind the object. This may be a tip-off that there is something up there when the kid is acting perfectly normal. When the object goes away, the smell goes away.

YOUR CHILD UNDER SIX MONTHS

Kids under six months can get colds, allergies and sinus infections just as older brothers and sisters do. A baby under six months old who has a cold for longer than a week should be seen by a doctor. That doesn't necessarily mean he will be treated, but he should be seen. We are always a little more careful with tiny babies.

We treat little ones carefully. We shun over-the-counter preparations, which can make babies irritable and cause irregular heartbeats. Instead, we tend to use saline drops, nasal aspirators and humidifiers to ease their stuffiness and runny noses.

The other thing we are more careful about in little ones is fever. Where a doctor would shrug off a one-year-old, or a four-year-old with a runny nose and a fever, with an infant we are a little more cautious. Consult your doctor if a fever develops in your runny-nose baby.

CHECKLIST

RUNNY NOSE WITH FEVER AND SNEEZING: Consider viral infection.

RUNNY NOSE WITH FEVER, COUGH AND SNEEZING THAT LASTS LONGER THAN TWO WEEKS UNINTERRUPTED: Consider sinus infection. Consult your physician.

RUNNY NOSE WITHOUT FEVER THAT PERSISTS: Consider allergy. Try to determine and remove cause.

RUNNY NOSE ASSOCIATED WITH SEASONS, PLACES, OR ANIMALS: Consider allergy. Try to determine and remove cause.

NOSEBLEED: Consider irritation and picking. Using the pinch method, try to stop the bleeding over two 15-minute periods. If unsuccessful, consult your physician.

RECURRENT NOSEBLEED: Consult your physician.

TREATMENT

Since runny noses in and of themselves aren't serious, we tend to want to let them run their course. Even if the child seems to be sick for almost the entire winter, we want to look carefully. If what we are dealing with is simply an endless succession of new colds, my tendency is to want to leave the child alone.

If behavior changes, and the child begins to act listless and sick; if circles appear under his eyes; if coughing begins to keep him, and you, up at night; if a fever associated with a cough lasts more than a day or two; if he starts to cry and appears to have the kind of pain that might make us suspect that the cold and runny nose has led to an ear infection—then and only then do I suggest that we begin to treat the child with antibiotics.

I feel the main problem with colds and runny noses is that we tend to overtreat them, not undertreat them. We don't want to put every kid on antibiotics because his nose has been running for ten days. It's misuse of the drug, which can reduce its effectiveness at a time when we do need to use it.

Similarly, I find that parents tend to over-use over-the-counter preparations when their child has a simple cold or runny nose. Too often parents simply spoon out decongestant cough syrup—or worse, one of the combination decongestant-antihistamine-cough suppressant syrups that have become popular—in the feeling that they should *do* something. What they are doing is causing a problem where there wasn't one before.

When you give a decongestant, it does help the symptoms while the child is taking it. But when you stop, it can have what we call a rebound effect. The body has gotten used to letting the decongestant do the work of controlling the mucus. When you take away the decongestant, then the body starts pouring out more mucus. That's the reason we tend to recommend using these types of remedies judiciously. Even though the label says they're safe to use every four to six hours or so, I find using them that often does run a good chance of creating a dependence on the decongestant, and a rebound reaction when you stop.

Most pediatricians say not to use this type of medication in children under six months of age. Some say under a year. Most of us agree that this symptom-controlling medication should be limited to the time of day when the symptoms are the worst. If you must give decongestants, then do it at night, when the cough is the worst and you and the child both need rest. My general advice, though, is to avoid using them at all if you can. If it's just a simple cough and runny nose, then let the condition run its course.

And get to think of his habit of wiping his nose on his sleeve as endearing.

SHALL I WAKE THE DOCTOR?

There are very few nose conditions that require waking up your doctor, or making a mad dash to the emergency room. A nosebleed that won't stop is one of them.

That means a nosebleed that, despite two 15-minute pinching sessions, is still flowing freely, or a nose that has been bleeding off and on all day and that begins to bleed profusely at night. That doesn't mean the kind of spotting that can be common following a nosebleed. That means significant, active bleeding.

Even nose trauma doesn't usually require immediate attention if it happens in the middle of the night. If the bleeding can be stopped, the problem can safely wait until morning. That's because kids' noses are generally softer than they are in adults. We don't usually get the kinds of broken noses that we see later on in adolescents and adults.

Of course if the nose does seem seriously misshapen or knocked to one side, or if the child is in inconsolable distress, by all means consult your physician.

CAN SHE GO TO SCHOOL?

Unless the child has an active fever, runny noses themselves are more an esthetic than a health problem. Some schools may ask children to stay out when their noses are actively running. My experience, though, is that schools who really enforce that rule run the risk of barring some children for most of the school year. My feeling is that when the kids are old enough, they should be taught good hygiene habits, like using tissues and coughing and sneezing into their elbows. But meantime, I don't find kids with runny noses a serious health hazard to other kids. Kids are going to get colds and runny noses all winter just from existing in the world with other people. Barring the kid with the runniest nose from school isn't going to make much of a dent in that situation.

ASK DR. JOHN

QUESTION: At first the stuff coming out of his nose was yellow, and now it's changed to a darkish green. Doesn't that mean it's more serious?

ANSWER: Most doctors still seem to agree that a change from a clear or milky discharge to a yellowish or greenish discharge is a possible sign of a change from a viral to a bacterial infection. But the color range within those two divisions of colors isn't really relevant. What's more, many doctors aren't even sure the color change makes a difference at all.

SKIN

Who doesn't remember it from his or her own childhood: the scratching and itching; the yucky-looking spots; the calamine lotion; the frustrating, futile attempts to reach a fist down the throat to get to that inaccessible itchy spot; and of course, the small compensating pleasures of as much ginger ale and Coke as you could drink, and unlimited access to daytime television. It's chicken pox, a rite of spring that sweeps schools everywhere. It's one of the most common of the childhood conditions whose most obvious symptom is **rash.**

When you talk about skin problems, it's rashes you are talking about. While most rashes are simple, others are among the most difficult things to diagnose. For one thing, there are so many different kinds and different causes, and the causes determine the treatment. In some cases, you treat the rash itself. In others, you ignore it and wait till the underlying disease goes away. But some are important indications of trouble.

There are rashes that are caused by bacterial infections of the skin. There are rashes caused by viral illnesses. There are rashes caused by contact with different substances, or by allergies or reactions to drugs. There are rashes caused either by insect bites directly or by the diseases the insects carry.

Another reason rashes are so hard to diagnose is that it's difficult to understand the guidelines. There are pictures in books, but somehow kids' rashes never seem to look like they do. Variations in skin color and tone make a big difference. In the end, you may wind up having your doctor take a look, but even experienced practitioners may have difficulties.

In this chapter I'll analyze rashes first by their appearance. Later I'll try to organize them by category. It's not simple, but I'll try to make this process as easy as possible. In the meantime, I'll give you a list of things to think about when you are looking at your child's rash.

One thing to keep in mind: We almost never see a serious condition that is signalled by a rash alone. Rashes that accompany serious disease almost always announce themselves through other symptoms like headache and high fever.

The first thing to do, even before you begin thinking about the rash itself, is ask yourself a few questions about your child and your current circumstances and activities. These are the kinds of questions I would ask my patients' parents immediately to see if we could get a hint about what may or may not be causing this rash.

First, ask yourself questions about your child and her activities just before the rash appeared:

- ❖ How old is the child?
- ❖ Has she had any recent immunizations?
- ❖ Has she been playing in new places?
- ❖ Has she been in or near fields or tall grass?
- ❖ Has she eaten or played with anything new?
- ❖ Has she had any contact with animals?
- ❖ Is there any illness going around her class?
- ❖ Does she have a fever?

Here's why we ask these questions. Knowing whether or not your child has a fever will help us distinguish those rashes caused by viruses and bacteria from those that only involve the surface of the skin.

I ask about the age of the child because there are certain rashes that are more common at certain ages. We rarely see **scarlet fever,** for example, in children under three or four years of age. We don't see **diaper rash,** of course, in children above diaper age.

There are also rashes that are simply known side effects of some immunizations, like the rash that follows the measles, mumps and rubella vaccine.

If your child has recently been playing in a new place, you might want to consider the rashes that are associated with insect bites. Mosquito bites on children can sometimes cause a larger, more generalized rash than just the familiar round, red, itchy spot. An allergic reaction to a bee sting can cause a rash all over the body.

Speaking of allergies, does your child have any known allergies? If you don't know of any, you might consider the possibility that she is developing one. Has she eaten large quantities of some unfamiliar food? Shellfish, citrus fruits, strawberries, even tomatoes can cause a child to break out in a rash. Similarly, playing with, wearing or using something new that comes in contact with the skin can cause rashes (a new detergent, soap, suntan lotion or shampoo, for example).

We ask about your child's friends because many illnesses that cause rashes come in waves, sometimes seeming like a local epidemic. Do you know through the grapevine that chicken pox has been running through your child's preschool? Do you know children with scarlet fever? Even if your child didn't play with that particular child, it spreads around. That's just the way kids are.

Now, let's consider what the rashes look like. These are the questions I would ask over the phone in trying to diagnose the rash.

- ❖ Is the rash itchy or not?
- ❖ Do you see the rash all over her body or just in one spot? What spot is it?
- ❖ Does the rash come and go, or is it there all day long?
- ❖ Does the rash have a pattern to it? Is it round? Blotchy? Pimply?
- ❖ Is the rash flat or filled with fluid?

In the following two sections, I will give you two ways to look at your child's rash. The first section will group the rashes by their two major categories: rashes without fevers and rashes with fevers. In the checklist, I'll organize it by the appearance of the rash. Looking through both sections should help give you a clue to your child's rash. **Remember: This is complicated. Check with your own doctor if you're in any doubt.**

RASHES WITHOUT FEVERS

Round, Red and Itchy:

If the rash is round, red, itchy and more or less permanent, there are three different causes you might consider. The first is **eczema.** Eczema is usually round, either in small or large patches, with a well-defined border. The entire patch will be red and scaly all over. It can be very itchy, and little kids will want to scratch it, increasing the redness. Eczema is fairly common. It can occur anywhere on the body, and can either be localized, that is in one spot only, or in patches all over the body. Frequently you'll find that other people in your family have had bouts with eczema, since it tends to run in families. Sometimes it is associated with allergies, especially allergies to milk. Usually, though, there is no cause that we can readily identify. Eczema is more common in the winter than in the summer, when skin dries out. We usually find that it will respond to some moisturizing lotion. In some cases, I might prescribe a mild cortisone cream to relieve the itching.

If, on the other hand, the rash is round and itchy, but has a clear patch in the center like a donut, then consider **ringworm.** Despite its unpleasant name, ringworm isn't caused by a worm at all. Rather, it is caused by a fungus. Because it is a fungal infection, we find that it doesn't respond to moisturizing cream or cortisone cream. Since ringworm and eczema can look a lot alike, that's one way we tell them apart—by what makes them go away. In a persistent case, your doctor can send a scraping out for a culture to determine if it is a fungus. But in most cases, that won't be necessary. If it is a fungus, it will clear up nicely with an application of one of the anti-fungal creams.

Another possible cause of round, red, itchy rashes could be **impetigo.** Impetigo can cause a circular lesion anywhere on the body. It starts out as a little red pimple, expands to the size of a dime, and then forms a crust and gets itchy. Then other spots crop up nearby and form the same pattern. Impetigo is a bacterial infection of the skin. We see it more in the summer than the winter. We often see impetigo where kids have scratched other cuts or insect bites, allowing bacteria to be introduced under the skin. Since this is caused by staph and strep bacteria, we find that impetigo, of course, doesn't respond to either moisturizer or to anti-fungal creams. Rather, we need to combat the bacterial infection with an antibiotic ointment. In more severe cases, we'll add an oral antibiotic to stop the spread of the infection.

Itchy with Blisters:

An itchy, red rash that can look like scratch marks with blisters along them could be **poison ivy.** If it's mild, the rash will appear only on one or two spots, the spots where the plant has touched the skin. In the more severe forms, with an extensive rash, there can be a generalized allergic reaction where the face turns bright red and swollen. You probably remember treating poison ivy with calamine lotion. The modern treatment, however, is to use a steroid cream and, in severe cases, an oral steroid. In its severe forms, poison ivy can debilitate a child for a while. But usually it's more an itchy nuisance than anything else.

Tiny, Itchy Spots with Severe Itching:

If you see lots of tiny pinpoint spots which seem to be itchy way out of proportion to the size of the spot then you should consider **scabies.** Scabies won't go away by itself. It is caused by tiny insects that bury themselves under the skin. It is contagious and must be treated with a special lotion.

Itchy Scalp:

If you notice your child persistently scratching her head, look closer. You may see little white flecks that look like grains of rice attached to the hair. These are called nits and are a sign of head **lice.** Sometimes you can actually see the live lice, which are tiny little bugs that jump. If your child gets sent home from school with a note saying that she has lice, don't be embarassed. Lice are extremely common, especially among school kids. Lice are very contagious. They have nothing to do with personal hygiene. Lice are a huge nuisance, though. You'll have to wash all your sheets, towels and pillowcases, and treat your child with a special shampoo. There are shampoos available both by prescription and over the counter. Generally, however, you won't need to see your doctor for this one, although you may want to vent your frustrations by calling him or her.

Round, Red, Itchy, Fleeting Spots:

Some day you may notice your child covered with round, red, itchy spots. They appear suddenly, last for a few hours, and then disappear of their own accord. There is no fever, and the child does not otherwise appear to be very sick. I would consider **hives,** and try to figure out the cause. Hives can look like a target, or be large and red. They can be all over the body, or just in a few spots. The main characteristic of hives is that they are raised and smooth, not scaly and crusty. They also don't stay around long. Frequently they are more prominent after a warm bath or shower. They can occur in children of any age, and at any time of year. We presume hives have some allergic cause, although they can also be associated with some infections, and in this case, might be accompanied by fever.

Usually, though, we look for an allergy. Sometimes parents are already aware of the child's allergy, like parents who know that their child is allergic to milk or strawberries. Sometimes we can figure it out by thinking back over what the child has eaten or touched in the previous few hours. Some common causes are shellfish, berries, peanuts, nuts and milk products. Animal dander can also cause hives in children who are sensitive. Perhaps you've made a recent visit to a petting zoo or had a relative visit with her Collie. Often it is difficult to determine the cause of hives, precisely because they are so fleeting. Sometimes a child will have a single episode of hives that clears up right away and never returns.

If the hives persist, or if they recur regularly, then we are more concerned. Start a diligent search to try to determine the cause, and ask parents to keep a record of the child's eating habits. While hives are almost always a benign condition, parents should watch closely to make sure that the hives are not followed by any other more serious symptoms.

Make sure that your child doesn't seem to be experiencing any swelling of the throat, choking or difficulty in breathing. If you see any sign of such difficulty, get your child to the emergency room as quickly as possible. She may need to be treated with intravenous medications to reduce the problems in the airway and aided in breathing if necessary.

Such reactions are very uncommon, especially given the prevalence of hives. But they do occur, and parents should be on the lookout. Common treatments for persistent cases of hives also include an oral antihistamine, which reduces the itching caused by the hives. One caution for parents: Unlike chicken pox, hives don't respond to warm baths with baking soda. In fact, warm baths make hives worse.

RASHES WITH FEVERS

Bull's-eye rash:
In the spring and summer, I often get phone calls that go like this:

> "Doctor, we've just been on vacation for a few days, and my child has been romping in the woods and in tall grass. Now she has a fever, and I'm worried about **Lyme disease.**"

The rash associated with Lyme disease is very distinctive. In fact, one parent recently said that it's like finding a sign stamped on your child that says "I have Lyme disease." It's a round, red rash that looks just like a target, that is, there is a center round spot, a ring of clear skin, then a donut-shaped red ring. It looks very much like an archery target, hence the informal name "bull's-eye rash."

Sometimes spider bites—especially the bite of the brown recluse spider which is very common all over the country—will give a rash that looks a little like a target. But that rash fades quickly. Not so the target rash of Lyme disease. The outer edges don't fade, but rather expand with time.

Lyme disease, named for the town in Connecticut where it first appeared, has now been identified in most of the Northeastern, and many midwestern and western states. Be alert for Lyme disease any time you've been in an area where it's prevalent. If you have removed a tick from your child recently, that would be an even clearer sign; but if you haven't, don't necessarily discount Lyme disease. You might easily have missed the tick. The ticks that carry this disease are tiny, about the size of the period at the end of this sentence. They are much smaller than the well-known dog tick. The rash starts out as a spot in the area where the tick was embedded. Then the ring spreads. Sometimes it is hard to see, especially if the tick is on the scalp of a child with long or thick hair.

In the summertime, also be alert for the other signs of Lyme disease. If your child is feverish with a headache, be sure to inspect her closely for the characteristic bull's-eye rash. The early symptoms of Lyme disease are much like those of the flu. Still in the summertime in areas known for Lyme disease, I would treat these symptoms very carefully, and not just shrug them off as another summer virus.

Lyme disease needs to be evaluated by a physician, who may order a blood test for confirmation. If Lyme disease is diagnosed, or even strongly suspected, your doctor will prescribe a course of antibiotics.

Redness All Over the Body:

There is one rash that is so pervasive that the whole body seems to grow red. This rash makes the skin rough, like sandpaper, and gives your child bright red cheeks. Even her tongue will be bright red and inflamed. With such a rash, you should consider **scarlet fever.**

Scarlet fever is caused by the streptococcus bacteria. Basically, it is a strep throat with a rash. With scarlet fever, you will usually notice the rash after you have noticed other symptoms. Scarlet fever usually begins with a fever, a headache and vomiting and a sore throat.

In the days before antibiotics, scarlet fever was a dreaded disease. These days, it is still a condition to take seriously since, now and then, a strep infection untreated by antibiotics can cause rheumatic fever which can cause heart damage. Fortunately, commonly-prescribed antibiotics are very effective against scarlet fever and strep throat.

Flat, Pinkish, Generalized Rash:

If your child first develops a very high fever (in the range of 104°) and then develops a flat, pinkish rash all over her body, consider **roseola.** There will be a high fever for three or four days, which drops and is followed by an outbreak of the rash. The rash and the fever don't occur at the same time. Because of the high fever, the child may not feel well and will probably be very cranky. This condition usually occurs in young kids between one and three years of age. Because roseola is caused by a virus, there is no special treatment beyond lowering the fever. (See the chapter on fever.)

Small Spots That Raise, Fill with Fluid, Then Pop:

It won't be hard for you to spot **chicken pox** coming. Chicken pox is a very contagious virus. You will almost certainly see other kids in her class, or her little playmates, all developing chicken pox at the same time.

Fortunately, except for the discomfort of the pox themselves, chicken pox is a fairly benign illness. Your child probably won't be very sick but can be uncomfortable and have mild fever, a little lethargy and some irritability.

What you will notice first are small, isolated spots that look like mosquito bites. You might notice a half dozen scattered spots on her back, chest or buttocks when you are bathing her. The small red spots then raise, fill with fluid, and then scrab over. Within a day or two of your noticing the first spots, they will pop out all over her body. They can appear on the face, the eyelids, the scalp, and the genitals. They come in clusters and are often very itchy. Little girls in particular can be bothered by itchy pox inside the vagina, just out of reach.

Sometimes the littler kids don't seem to mind even the itching. But if they do, there are several ways to alleviate their discomfort. Commercial oatmeal-bath preparations are soothing (although they are very messy and slippery in the bathtub). Cheaper, cleaner and just as effective is a bath into which you dump a half cup of baking soda. Applications of a baking soda paste onto the itchy pox themselves can help; so can daubing the pox with calamine lotion. An antihistamine like Benadryl, given by mouth, can help reduce itching.

To prevent the worst of the scratching, which can lead to infections, keep fingernails cut short and hands clean. At night, you could try to make them wear gloves to bed, or put band-aids over their fingertips. As a reassurance: While small scars may remain for many months after the chicken pox have passed, those marks rarely remain there over the long term and almost never persist into adulthood. The whole illness lasts from five to seven days.

"Slapped Cheek" Rash:

The first thing you will notice is a flaming red rash on your child's cheeks. The striking appearance of the rash is what leads us to call it a slapped cheek rash. This is so-called **fifth disease,** so named because it was the fifth rash illness described in children. Kids with fifth disease also have a low fever, no appetite, lethargy and a runny nose. Sometimes you will see a generalized lacy rash all over the child's body, but the characteristic flaming cheeks are the tip-off.

We generally see fifth disease mini-epidemics among young school-age children. It is caused by a virus. It's not a serious illness and requires no special treatment beyond making sure the child is comfortable.

If you see tiny, pinpoint red or reddish brown spots anywhere on your child's body, press on them to see if they blanch to the touch. If not, seek immediate medical attention. Such spots could be a symptom of **meningococcemia,** a bacterial infection that can affect blood or cause meningitis. That is a life-threatening condition. While these spots are rare, they should be evaluated immediately even in the absence of other signs, since the spots can sometimes appear before other symptoms like fever or headache.

YOUR CHILD UNDER SIX MONTHS

Newborn babies' skin goes through all kinds of changes in the first few weeks of life. Because of this, rashes and other skin conditions are very common. Most of them are benign, untroubling symptoms that disappear on their own as the baby's skin gets used to its new existence out in the world. Only a few of them require treatment.

Flaky, peeling skin occurs almost universally during the first two to four weeks. You notice it most prominently on the backs of the hands and wrists and on the ankles. Such flaking and peeling is just part of the normal transition of baby skin from its life in the amniotic fluid to life in the open air. The skin can become red and cracked, but usually no treatment beyond lotion is necessary.

Sometimes parents will see little whiteheads on their newborn's body. The area surrounding the little whitehead will be red, and may be as big as a dime. There are two possible causes. If the whiteheads are fleeting—that is, if they disappear by the time your doctor calls you back, and then reappear in another spot just after she hangs up—then your baby probably has **E. toxicum.** E. toxicum, is also known informally as "flea bites," although it has nothing to do with fleas. We don't actually know what causes it. We do know that it's a benign condition that just comes and goes.

If the whitehead stays in one place, however, and grows bigger than a pinpoint, it could be **pustulosis.** Pustulosis requires treatment. The small, pus-filled blisters usually appear in the diaper area. It means that some bacteria, usually staphylococcus, has gotten under your baby's skin, causing an infection. This condition is potentially a serious one and requires a doctor's attention.

This condition used to be much more common than it is now. One reason we don't see much of it any more is that babies are sent home from the hospital quickly, and thus spend less time in hospital nurseries being handled by many different people. The more widespread use of antibiotic soap for handwashing also helps. If you see pinhead spots, however, the way to tell a serious condition from a benign one is to watch the spot closely: A spot that vanishes quickly and reappears in another place is harmless. One that stays in place and grows is not.

Another pimple-like rash that appears on babies' faces may remind parents of their own adolescence. In fact, these little whiteheads and blackheads that cluster on newborns' faces are called **infantile acne.** They are a little more common in boys than girls. This kind of acne, however, always goes away by itself within a few months without treatment and never leaves scars.

In dark-skinned babies we see another type of pimple-like rash. It starts off with a little pustule, a little bigger than a pimple, that develops on the baby's third or fourth day of life. That pustule then disappears and is replaced by a little brown spot where the pustule was. It is called **pustular melanosis.** No one knows what causes it, but it goes away on its own, and without scarring.

Sometimes parents will notice red pimples on their newborn's face and forehead, sometimes on the neck, and on the scalp. The pimples then give way to flaky patches that look like dandruff. Then the flakes build up into hard patches. This is a condition known as **cradle cap** or **seborrhea.** It isn't serious, but it is unsightly. Fortunately, it's easy to treat. Baby oil rubbed into the child's scalp, left to sit for a few hours and then washed out with baby shampoo, usually does the trick. Only occasionally do I have to prescribe some kind of medicated shampoo for a child.

Diaper Rash:

Diaper rash is almost universal in babies in the first year of life, and often beyond that as long as the child is in diapers. There is a lot of controversy these days about whether diaper rash is more common in babies who wear cloth or disposable diapers. But I feel it isn't the material itself that's at issue, though, since diaper rash isn't generally caused by contact with a fabric, but rather from the irritation of the skin from stools and urine. Sometimes diaper rash will come on suddenly, and be associated with the introduction of some new foods.

Ordinary diaper rash will respond to a little extra care. If you use baby wipes, then use water afterwards to sponge off the area. When cleaning the baby, use a mild soap, or no soap at all. Use a diaper ointment, to provide a barrier between the wet diaper and the baby's bottom. And, if you can stand it, air out the baby's skin as much as possible. Letting the baby lie around for extended periods of time without a diaper will work wonders on diaper rash, although it might not be good for your upholstery.

Sometimes, however, parents will come across a rash on the bottom that just won't go away. In that case, I would consider a **fungal rash,** also called **yeast infection.** Check the rash carefully. An ordinary diaper rash will be non-specific, with either small, pimple-like spots all over the area, or a redness that fades in and out of the normal skin, with no specific borders. The yeast infection, or fungal rash, however, is much more specific. It has a very well-demarcated border, and is raised. Often, there are angry-looking little spots, called satellite spots, around it. Typically, you will have treated this rash as a diaper rash for several days without any success. That's because the ordinary creams that soothe a diaper rash won't attack the fungus that causes this kind of rash. Because fungus thrives in a dark, warm, moist condition, it will wither away and die in the light. Thus, the diaper-off method will work particularly well for fungus. Let the baby lie around for a few days minus diaper, and the problem is solved. Most parents, though, can't risk their furniture that way. Thus, I would suggest a call to the physician for an anti-fungal cream that will work just as well.

Sometimes parents will notice little ulcerations of the skin, usually around the rectum. This usually means there is a superficial **bacterial skin infection.** It's found strictly around the rectal area, and can be caused by very acidic stools, or from some bacteria that has managed to get into the skin. This condition is much less common than the run-of-the-mill diaper rash or fungal infections. It responds to an antibiotic ointment.

Occasionally, little babies will get a more serious skin infection, one that looks like great big blisters all over the skin. The child's skin will look scalded, with big, water-filled blisters, called **bullae.** That means that a staphylococcal bacteria has invaded the skin. This is something that requires immediate medical attention because of the potential seriousness of such an infection.

CHECKLIST

What Does the Rash Look Like?

ROUND, RED, ITCHY AND MORE OR LESS PERMANENT WITH NO FEVER: Consider eczema, impetego, or ringworm.

ROUND, RED, ITCHY AND RAISED USUALLY WITHOUT FEVER: Consider hives.

BULL'S-EYE RASH WITH EXPANDING BORDER WITH FEVER AND BODY ACHES AND FLU-LIKE SYMPTOMS, HEADACHE: Consider Lyme disease.

RED FLUSH ALL OVER THE BODY WITH FEVER AND SORE THROAT: Consider scarlet fever.

FLAT PINKISH RASH ALL OVER THE BODY AFTER THE DISAPPEARANCE OF A VERY HIGH FEVER THAT HAS LASTED THREE TO FOUR DAYS, OFTEN IN A CHILD BETWEEN 1 AND 4 YEARS OF AGE: Consider roseola.

RED SPOTS THAT LOOK LIKE MOSQUITO BITES AND ITCHY RAISED SPOTS THAT FILL WITH FLUID IN A USUALLY HEALTHY-LOOKING KID OF PRESCHOOL AGE, OR ONE WITH OLDER SIBLINGS. Consider chicken pox.

FLAT RED CHRONIC RASHES THAT ARE SCALY AND ITCHY AND LAST FOR A WHILE: Consider eczema.

RED RAISED, ITCHY, SPOTS THAT FOLLOW A NEW DRUG OR VACCINATION OR CONTACT WITH A NEW ANIMAL: Consider hives.

CHECKLIST FOR BABIES

PIMPLE-LIKE RED SPOTS ON THE BOTTOM AND AROUND GENITALS: Consider diaper rash.

REDDISH, WELL-DEFINED RASH ON BOTTOM AND AROUND GENITALS WITH WELL-DEFINED BORDERS THAT DOESN'T RESPOND TO DIAPER RASH TREATMENT: Consider fungus.

RASHES YOU GOT THAT YOUR CHILD WON'T GET

I still get these calls all the time:
"Doctor, I think she's got the measles."
"Doctor, I think she's got rubella."
Guess what?
She probably doesn't have any of those things. These illnesses were so much a part of our own childhood landscapes that they've been somehow indelibly imprinted in our memories. The fact is, though, that measles and rubella—and a whole host of other once-common childhood diseases—are a thing of the past for most children.

Immunizations for many of these illnesses are now required for school admission all over the United States. As a result, it's a pretty safe bet that your child won't get measles, mumps, rubella (otherwise known as German measles) or whooping cough. Very soon, an immunization against chicken pox will also be available.

SHALL I WAKE THE DOCTOR?

Call your doctor immediately—at any time of the day or night—if your child has hives associated with wheezing, choking, and coughing. The hives alone aren't enough. It's the respiratory distress that indicates a swelling in the throat. If a child has a hive rash and is having trouble swallowing, it is generally because of an allergic reaction. Such a reaction is uncommon, but it is dangerous. If you can't reach your doctor, go to the emergency room.

You should also seek immediate medical attention if you see anywhere on your child's body tiny, pinpoint red or reddish brown spots that don't blanch to the touch. That could signal **meningococcemia,** a life-threatening infection.

CAN SHE GO BACK TO SCHOOL?

Lice: After treatment begins.

Eczema/ringworm/impetigo: After treatment begins. (Eczema isn't contagious. Ringworm and impetigo are only mildly contagious.)

Poison ivy: Any time, as long as she feels all right. (Despite your childhood memories of the other kids on the playground threatening to rub their poison ivy on you, the poison ivy rash isn't contagious. It's a reaction to the oil on the plant. By the time the rash appears a day or two after exposure, the oil has usually been well washed off.)

Scabies: After treatment begins.

Chicken pox: After all the spots have crusted. (This is usually five to seven days from the outset of the illness.)

Fifth disease: Any time. (By the time the rash appears, the child is no longer contagious, so if she is feeling up to it, she doesn't need to miss any school at all.)

Lyme disease: Lyme disease isn't contagious, so if she is feeling well, you can send her back to school any time.

ASK DR. JOHN

QUESTION: I have bad scars on my face from the acne I had as a teenager. My new baby has acne all over her face. Isn't she going to be scarred from this?

ANSWER: No. Infantile acne isn't scarring, nor is it associated with an increased risk of teenage acne.

QUESTION: I've kept my child indoors for several days while she had chicken pox, but finally I couldn't stand it any longer, and took her to the playground. The other mothers all looked at me funny. When is it safe for her to play with other kids?

ANSWER: Chicken pox is no longer contagious by the time the spots all crust over. That will occur between five and seven days from the onset of the illness. There's no need to isolate children until the spots disappear. That's a good thing, too, because the spots can sometimes last for weeks after the actual illness has passed.

QUESTION: I notice that the tip of my little boy's penis is quite red. Is this a problem?

ANSWER: This isn't usually a problem. If the child is fussing or has a fever, it might be a sign of infection, which does require a doctor's attention. But usually I find that it results simply from a non-specific irritation, which can be treated with an over-the-counter ointment like Bacitracin. You should also try to locate the cause of the irritation, perhaps in a new detergent used to wash his clothes. Bubblebath is another common culprit.

QUESTION: My child has had Lyme disease. What kind of problems is this going to cause for her in the future?

ANSWER: In adults, the long-term consequences of Lyme disease can be severe, including a chronic arthritis-like condition and fatigue. In children, however, the good news is that most research so far shows no such long-term consequences. Properly treated with antibiotics, it appears that most children completely recover from Lyme disease.

QUESTION: Which of the rashes are contagious?
ANSWER: Among the most common are chicken pox, scarlet fever, impetigo, and to a lesser extent, ringworm.

URINATION

Kids pee a lot!

What's more, parents have a lot of contact with their kids' urine, especially when the children are in diapers. So parents are very sensitive to any changes in the color and smell of their child's urine, and to changes in their habits. As children grow, their urinary habits—both day and night—change quite rapidly. Some of these changes indicate an illness; many of them do not.

Children can experience a sudden change in the frequency with which they urinate. Usually it's an increase in frequency that parents notice, when it begins to seem as if she needs to go to the bathroom every ten minutes. Occasionally, although this is less frequent, parents notice that the child hardly seems to be urinating at all. Kids can also complain that urinating hurts. They can appear uncomfortable. Even more common, a toilet-trained child can suddenly appear to be dribbling all day long, or not quite making it to the bathroom.

Another urinary problem isn't usually an illness, but it's worrisome to parents all the same: bedwetting. Every year I get dozens of calls about it.

All these urinary problems are upsetting to parents. At the

same time, they have another dimension to them that many other childhood illnesses do not: Urinary problems can be troublesome and disruptive to a household. Bedwetting, for example, can be as much or more of a problem for the parents who must deal with the midnight bed puddles as for the child who creates them.

Most parents, I believe, instinctively recognize the reality of urinary problems. Changes in urinary patterns alone may not signal medical problems. Fever is the key. If a child has urinary difficulty and fever, we take it more seriously. That, in fact, is cause for a midnight call to your doctor, or a quick trip to the emergency room. High or persistent fever, without other symptoms, would also lead us to look for an infection in the urinary tract.

But what about a child who somehow just can't seem to make it to the bathroom? Or one who starts wetting his pants every day, but only when he's at school? Or one who at age five is still not dry at night? Or at age seven? Or one who has been dry at night and then suddenly begins wetting again? All these are puzzles, and the problem is figuring out how much of the problem is medical and how much is emotional.

So ask yourself the following questions:

- ❖ Does the child have fever?
- ❖ Does the child appear sick or well?
- ❖ Is she uncomfortable?
- ❖ Is she in pain?
- ❖ Is she peeing more or less often?
- ❖ Is she complaining of burning or itching?
- ❖ Has something stressful recently happened in her life?
- ❖ Is the change in urine habits in the daytime only or does it happen both day and night?

The answers to these questions will give us a way to evaluate her urinary problems. The most important of these questions relates to fever. Fever can be an important clue to **urinary tract infections.** True urinary tract infections in children aren't anywhere near as common as the other conditions we will discuss. But urinary tract infections can be very serious and do require rapid medical attention. So skip right to the "Increased frequency with Fever" section of this chapter if you suspect a urinary tract infection.

So now let's look at the four major complaints in order of their occurence in kids: increased frequency, pain on urination, fever, and change in color.

INCREASED FREQUENCY—NO PAIN, NO FEVER

A common change in urinary habits in children is an **increase in frequency**. The reasons aren't always illness. Even when they are not in pain, children sometimes develop a need to pee more frequently than usual, or so suddenly that they don't quite make it to the bathroom. First we want to make sure there really is no pain or discomfort. Then we want to make sure there is no fever. If the only thing you notice is that he is making the round trip to the bathroom a couple of times an hour—or if the teacher is complaining about the same thing—then we start looking for other causes.

One of the first things we would consider in urinary frequency without pain is **anxiety.** There are all kinds of situations that can make a child need to urinate frequently or suddenly. Kids who are anxious at school and want to get out of class can begin urinating frequently. A parent leaving on a business trip can do it. So can a sibling getting sick. Basically, anything that upsets a child's routine can affect urination. A "wonderful" event like the birth of a sibling can so unsettle a child that she may begin wetting herself again.

So we first need to consider when she is doing the wetting. Is it only during the school week, or perhaps only at school? Has she recently had any upsetting events in her life? Is she having conflicts with a teacher or parent? One thing to check is nighttime dryness. If she wets during the day, but remains dry during the night, then her problem is probably emotional. A child with a **urinary tract infection,** or some medical problem, has trouble holding urine both day and night.

Because urinary tract infections aren't uncommon, and can lead to more serious problems, I still recommend that kids with increased frequency and no other symptoms come to the office for a urine culture to rule out infections. We'll discuss infections and irritation later in the chapter.

Pinworms can also cause urinary frequency, especially in girls. Pinworms are parasites that are found in the lower intestine. They crawl out of the anus and can migrate into a girl's urethra— especially if she is diaper-age—causing irritation or frequency. We don't find this problem much in boys, because of the longer length of the urethra. The most common symptom of pinworms, however, is rectal itching.

If your child has urinary frequency both day and night, has no fever, but wants to drink excessively—more often than every hour or so—you should consider **diabetes.** Your child also might lose her appetite, or have an otherwise unexplainable weight loss. Juvenile diabetes is uncommon, but if you suspect it, be sure to consult your doctor. He or she will test for sugar in the urine and do a blood test.

One last thing: It isn't your imagination. A leading cause of urinary frequency is **cars.** My own kids have taught me that. Put a kid anywhere near a car, and she'll need to go almost immediately. And then over and over and over again. **Gas stations and rest stops** also cause a need to urinate: Just as soon as you drive past, all your kids will instantly need to go. What's the solution? Beats me. Write me if you find out.

INCREASED FREQUENCY—WITH PAIN, BUT NO FEVER

"It hurts when I make wee wee!"

Your child may complain—using whatever words are common in your family vocabulary—that it hurts to urinate. You might find your child, boy or girl, grabbing the genital area in an attempt to get at the pain. They may cry or say their genitals burn or sting; they may wriggle, or make gestures that indicate that their genitals itch. In addition, they may complain of a stomach ache.

The pain or discomfort may be so great that your child may have frequent attacks of a sudden need to urinate. In fact the frequency of urination may be much greater than usual—say, several times an hour—and the quantity urinated each time may be much smaller than usual. That's because the burning or itching sensation mimics the need to urinate, when in fact the bladder isn't actually full. On the other hand in some cases, especially with girls, the pain may be so great that she will refuse to urinate at all.

Sometimes a child will have a greatly increased frequency of urination, and will show signs of pain or irritation, but will not have a fever. As I mentioned earlier, we always rule out bladder infections, so I would always recommend that a child complaining of pain on urination have her urine tested for bacteria.

In most cases, however, in the absence of a fever, I would consider that pain on urination is caused by an **irritated urethra.** Both boys and girls suffer from this condition. It is easier to diagnose in a boy than a girl because you will be able to see the redness at the end of his penis. With an irritated urethra, the child will be very uncomfortable, but there won't be any actual infection. We may do a urine culture anyway just to make sure. The treatment, however, consists of a local cortisone cream to reduce the irritation. Sitting for a while in warm (not soapy) water will also help to relieve the discomfort. Antibiotics aren't needed, because there isn't any true infection.

There is one big culprit we often find in cases of irritated urethra: bubble baths, especially for girls. They seem innocent enough, but bubble baths actually cause a great deal of harm. Bubblebath is extremely irritating to children's (and adults'!) urinary systems. Even sitting in a tub full of soapy water can be irritating. When you bathe your child, soap her last. Shampoo her last. And be cautious using bubblebath.

INCREASED FREQUENCY WITH FEVER

If a child has increased frequency of urination or complains of pain on urination and also has a fever, I would consider a diagnosis of **urinary tract infection.** One such infection is caused when bacteria travel up the urinary tract from the urethra, which is the opening of the urinary tract to the outside of the body. We call the condition a **bladder infection,** but the fact is that other parts of the urinary tract can become infected with bacteria as well.

Urinary tract infections are much more common in girls than in boys. The reason is that girls' urethras are much shorter than boys', giving the bacteria a much shorter route to travel before it can cause an infection. In girls, urinary tract infections are fairly common. In boys, they are fairly unusual. In fact, whenever I see a true urinary tract infection in a boy, I will usually want to examine him to see if there is some anatomical abnormality.

We diagnose urinary tract infections by doing a urine culture in which we look for signs of bacteria in the urine. Often, however, the symptoms are so evident, and the child is in such discomfort, that I will start the child on a course of antibiotics before the culture even returns from the laboratory. The treatment, in any case, consists of antibiotics that are particularly effective against infections in the urinary tract.

If the child, however, has a high fever—that is, one that spikes as high as 105° or 106° and can't be brought down—and looks lethargic and acts listless, we want to take some immediate action. The confusing part for parents is that often this high, spiking fever can mean a serious **kidney infection** even if the child isn't complaining of urinary problems. Read the "Fever" chapter for more information on the different types of fevers and what they mean.

Such a high fever combined with complaints of urinary difficulties or lower back or "tummy" pain should send you right to your doctor or to the emergency room. Kidney infections aren't common, but they aren't rare either. They are also more serious than bladder infections, which can sometimes be viral and mild. Kidney infections can lead to blood infections, and a very, very sick kid.

Fever plus urinary complaints: Call the doctor.

High, spiking fever and a listless kid: Call the doctor.

URINARY RETENTION

A urinary tract infection can lead to **urinary retention,** as the child voluntarily withholds urine because of the memory of the pain the last time she went to the bathroom. I will get calls from parents who say their child went from complaining about burning and hurting on urination to refusing to urinate at all and complaining of tummy pain. My solution? I tell them to put her in a warm bath and tell her it's okay to pee in the water. That seems to relieve the discomfort enough to allow her to urinate.

CHANGE IN COLOR

The first thing parents naturally think when their child's urine changes color is "Blood!" That's especially logical because the color usually changes towards a more red or orange hue. But while that color change suggests to parents the presence of blood in the urine, in fact changing color isn't a good indication of blood in the urine. It is true that infections, can and do irritate the urinary tract or the bladder enough to cause tiny amounts of blood to appear in the urine. But this blood is usually in such a small quantity as to be invisible, or nearly so, to the naked eye. In fact blood is one of the signs of bacterial infection and we do a urinalysis to detect it.

A change in color instead is very likely to be the result of **ingestion.** In other words, it's something she ate or drank.

It's a phenomenon that should be familiar to most adults. Many things we eat or drink pass through their effects to the urine.

In children a change in urine color may be due to any number of things. Some food colorings can change the urine's color. So can red or purple Jello. Black currant juice is another possible culprit. B-vitamins, or multiple vitamins containing large amounts of vitamin B, will change the urine to a deep yellow or orange color. Beets, if you can get your child to eat them, will dye urine a bright red. There is even a name for this condition: beeturia. It isn't a serious problem and in fact, I believe most parents would count themselves lucky if they had a child who was willing to eat enough beets to show up in the urine.

A change in urine color can also be a sign that the child has eaten something he shouldn't have. One mother called up one weekend and said her son's urine had turned a bright orange. Before I asked to see him, I asked the mother if she had any pyridium in the house. (That's a drug that women use for urinary pain.) Sure enough one of her two remaining tablets was missing. Monday morning we sent the child for a urine test just to be sure. The test, of course, was negative, and the urine returned quickly to its normal color.

If the urine has changed color because of ingestion, I usually just ask parents to wait until the dyeing effect wears off. If the child pees red, and there is no evidence that he's eaten something that might be responsible, we will order a urine test just to make sure. But usually we find that time clears it up.

BEDWETTING

Bedwetting is one of the most common urinary problems we face. And for parents, I must say, it's most annoying. I get calls from concerned parents all the time.

> "Doctor, she's four-and-a-half years old, and she's still not dry at night. . . ." Or, "Doctor, he's five years old and I'm getting tired of getting up to get him clean sheets three times a week. . . ."

I agree that bedwetting is extremely troublesome, not to mention hazardous to a parent's good night's sleep. It can be even more of a nuisance when you have more than one child. If one isn't by your bedside plaintively complaining of a cold, soggy bed, then the other one is.

There are two kinds of bedwetting: bedwetting in a child who has never been dry and bedwetting in a child who has been dry at night but who starts to wet again. The first kind of bedwetting is extremely common. In my experience, most parents worry about it too soon. Medically we don't even define this kind of bedwetting as a problem until after six years of age. Before that, we just chalk it up to slow but not abnormal development.

In fact, although our rule-of-thumb statistics say that 90% of children are dry by age six, I always point out to parents that means that 10% of them aren't. Those one in ten children who still wet the bed by age six are just children who, for one reason or another, are at the far end of the bell curve of normal childhood development in this regard.

Still, I get calls from parents who are exhausted, tired of getting up and worried about what it might mean. If a parent is worried, I will do a urine culture and check for any problems. Do I ever find them? Never.

What causes bedwetting? There probably is no one single cause. Often we will find there is a family history of bedwetting. Parents will remember that their siblings, or even they themselves, wet the bed until quite late. Perhaps some kids have small bladders, and can't hold their urine as long as other kids. Some kids may have a delay in the maturing of the neurological feedback that gives them the signal from the bladder to the brain that it's time to get up. Some kids may just be exceptionally sound sleepers. Parents will often report to me that their child wets the bed, but doesn't even notice it, and will sleep the rest of the night in a puddle if the parent doesn't intervene.

After age six, bedwetting can become a social problem for a child. With kids starting sleep-overs, or maybe even starting to think about sleep-away camp, wetting the bed can become embarrassing for a child. So if parents consult me, I generally recommend that after age six they begin trying some things to help the child increase nighttime control.

The simplest is giving the child a head start on the night. Many parents—myself included—find that their child can make it through the night with a little boost. So get her up for one final pee just before you go to bed. Some parents think it's unkind to wake a sleeping child just for a bathroom run. But from my own experience as a parent I can tell you that they never notice it: Kids can pee in their sleep.

Sometimes a little practice holding urine can help. During the day, ask your child to wait a few minutes past the time she thinks she needs to urinate. We call it "bladder stretching". Some parents also try behavior modification, the same technique you use to try to get her to clean her room. Stars on a chart, promises of a treat at the end of a dry week—some parents find this works.

If none of these behavior modification techniques works you may want to try a little more drastic measure. There are a variety of alarm systems available commercially. Pharmacies carry them or know how to order them.

In my experience they are very effective in treating bedwetting. They aren't harmful to the child, and they do the trick quickly. The alarms have a trigger system. As soon as the pad underneath the kid gets slightly wet, an alarm goes off. It wakes the child, and as soon as the child awakes, she stops peeing immediately. It's a kind of Pavlovian response. It usually takes two or three months for the response to become firmly fixed, but once it works, it works.

Some doctors prescribe medications. The drug of choice is a hormonal nasal spray that reduces urine production. There may be a very small minority of children who need the medication but I've never had to prescribe it. The alarms work so well I've never needed it. From my point of view, however, the major problem is that once the medication is stopped, the bedwetting is likely to recur, whereas an alarm-trained child is frequently dry for good.

Don't worry about the alarms traumatizing the kid for life. In my experience the child is so delighted to be dry at night, that she doesn't seem to object. In any case, a year or so later she's completely forgotten the experience.

Secondary bedwetting is another matter. That's when a previously dry child suddenly begins wetting the bed again. I'll give even the dryest kid one accident once in a while, but if it happens more than once I'll ask to see the child. It's possibly an early sign of diabetes, or of a bladder infection. I'll want to test the child's urine for sugar and for signs of an infection.

One other common cause of secondary bedwetting is emotional. Did something happen in her life? Some stress at school? Did she lose a pet? Emotional traumas can cause a temporary recurrance of bedwetting.

SEXUAL ABUSE

With all the attention given to sexual abuse these days, it's natural that parents become concerned about it when anything goes wrong with anything that involves their child's genitals. I often get hesitant calls from concerned parents: "Am I just being paranoid, or. . . ."

Indeed, urinary tract disturbances may in fact be one of the signs we have that point to sexual abuse. That said, let me make it clear: Urinary tract infections are common. Most of them occur as a result of the ways bacteria can make its way into the system that I discussed earlier. What's more, because such infections are so common, an infection alone would almost never be a reason for us to suspect sexual abuse.

Urinary retention, which as I said earlier is uncommon, is one sign that might lead us to think about the possibility of sexual abuse. That's because sexual abuse can cause an irritation of the urethral opening that is so painful that the child refuses to urinate.

Still, as with the other conditions we have discussed throughout this book, **changes in behavior** are key to our thinking about sexual abuse. There won't be a single symptom that will necessarily raise a red flag, but rather a number of different things. We might find changes in appetite. An increase in fearfulness, wakefulness and nightmares. There might be a refusal to go somewhere that the child once went willingly. There might be some change in apparent personality, as when a normally docile child becomes belligerent, or an active, outgoing child becomes withdrawn.

The investigation of sexual abuse by a hospital team is massive and thorough, and includes interviews by doctors, social workers and experts in sexual abuse.

YOUR CHILD UNDER SIX MONTHS

One of the first panicked calls from parents of newborns often has to do with the baby's urine. In the first few days of life, a baby's urine may turn salmon-colored, or rust-colored. Because of the dramatic **color change,** parents think their newborn is urinating blood.

That isn't the case. Newborns' urine contains crystals of a chemical called oxalate which causes that color change. It is very common, and not a cause for alarm.

Babies do get urinary tract infections. But diagnosing a baby's urinary tract infection is more complicated than with an older child. That's because the most obvious symptom—pain on urination—isn't as obvious in a little baby. Where the older child will make her complaint known, a baby will simply cry. With tiny babies who cry or have fevers that we can't explain in any other way, we will consider a urinary tract infection. The baby will be fitted with a tiny bag to collect the urine for testing.

The most serious symptom is a **high, spiking fever.** As we discussed in the chapter on fever, many fevers in infants should be immediately investigated. Urinary tract infections may in fact be the cause, but often enough that isn't apparent until *after* medical tests are done.

In babies and young children with proven urinary tract infections, we become concerned that the cause may be an anatomical defect, especially if the baby is a boy. Still, such defects are uncommon in both boys and girls and can only be diagnosed by special x-ray tests or ultrasound.

CHECKLIST

URINE CHANGES COLOR: Think of what your child may have eaten. Some common causes are beets, food coloring, B-vitamins and some medications.

PAIN ON URINATION (WITH FEVER): Consider a urinary tract infection. Call your doctor.

PAIN ON URINATION (NO FEVER): Consider an irritated urethra, or possibly pinworms. Call your doctor.

URINARY FREQUENCY (WITH PAIN AND WITH FEVER): Consider a urinary tract infection. Call your doctor.

URINARY FREQUENCY (WITH PAIN AND NO FEVER): Consider irritated urethra. Call your doctor.

URINARY FREQUENCY (NO PAIN AND NO FEVER): Consider anxiety or some emotional problem.

URINARY FREQUENCY (WITH EXCESSIVE THIRST AND WEIGHT CHANGE): Consider diabetes.

SHALL I WAKE THE DOCTOR?

If your child experiences high fever, chills and burning on urination, call your doctor immediately, day or night. These are among the signs that doctors take most seriously because they could be signs of **kidney infection.** Kidney infections are rare, but because they can very quickly develop into serious, life-threatening conditions, we take them seriously and treat the symptoms immediately.

How do you know that you should be concerned? If your child has no sign of a fever, pain or burning on urination alone shouldn't concern you in the middle of the night. It's the combination of fever and burning on urination that should concern you, or a high fever that won't respond to acetaminophen. If the child wakes in the middle of the night with a high fever but no other symptoms, or with cold symptoms only, try acetaminophen, as we suggest in the "Fever chapter." If the fever subsides, and the child appears more comfortable and ready for sleep or play, you can relax. If the acetaminophen causes the fever to drop only a little, and the child still feels uncomfortable, or acts sick, it's better to be safe. Call the doctor.

Kidney infections can make a child very sick in a big hurry. There are antibiotics available these days which can be injected, and which are very effective against the bacteria that cause these infections.

Another reason to seek immediate medical attention is if your child begins to pee **bright red blood.** That is a possible sign of kidney damage that requires attention. In this case, we don't mean minor or faint alterations in color, but a change that you can clearly identify as blood. If you can't reach the doctor, head for the emergency room.

CAN SHE GO BACK TO SCHOOL?

How quickly the child can return to school depends on the nature of the problem that kept her out in the first place. If your child has had a serious urinary tract infection, she will have been pretty ill. So you should consult with your doctor before sending her back to school. Usually I would suggest waiting a day or two after the fever has subsided and she is up and about again.

Urinary tract conditions—from irritation to true infections—aren't contagious. So your concern is for the child's comfort and the convenience of the teacher. A child who is missing the bathroom two or three times a day isn't going to be a happy child, whether or not he is pronounced non-contagious and ready for school.

If you have determined that your child's wetting problem is caused by anxiety, it's best not to avoid school, but to try to address the problem. In my experience, the things that make children anxious aren't major things, and can be dealt with relatively easily. I've found that things like scary movies or hearing about someone who is sick are leading causes of anxiety.

ASK DR. JOHN

QUESTION: When I had a urinary tract infection, the doctor gave me not only antibiotics, but also a pain-killing drug. My child is so uncomfortable. Isn't there something I can do for her?

ANSWER: We don't use pain-killing drugs on children. If they have a true infection, children respond very quickly to antibiotics and the pain rapidly subsides. A warm bath can help the discomfort if there are retention problems.

QUESTION: My little boy is six years old and he's still not dry at night. Is this a problem?

ANSWER: A problem for whom? In cases of bedwetting, how aggressively we treat it depends a good deal on who it is that is inconvenienced and how strongly they feel about it. The vast majority of bedwetting cases aren't caused by illness or anatomical abnormalities.

VOMITING

It certainly isn't as romantic as some possible pairings and it doesn't rhyme with horse and carriage. But there's still no doubt about it: vomiting and diarrhea do go together.

That's why I suggest that you read the "Diarrhea" chapter. Many of the causes of diarrhea are also the most likely causes of vomiting. Then you might want to read the "Fever" chapter too. Because the single biggest cause of both vomiting and diarrhea is **viral gastroenteritis—the stomach flu.**

Usually the first call I get will be about the vomiting. The parent has had to come get the child at school where she's thrown up her lunch. By the time Mom or Dad arrives, the child is running a fever. The diarrhea often follows within 24 hours as the virus works its way through the intestinal tract.

These viruses can occur in either summer or winter. Because these viruses are passed from person to person, you'll find that half her class will be suffering the same complaint before too long. And so, perhaps, will you.

Vomiting with the same pattern as the flu can mean **food poisoning.** The most common types of food poisoning are staphyloccocal and salmonella. In any case, the differences are usually academic. If there is a major outbreak at an institution, a school or a day-care center, for example, physicians may order stool cultures and other tests to determine the origin. But that's usually for prevention purposes, to identify the source of the outbreak and to remove it. In young children, flu is far more common than food poisoning. Sometimes antibiotics are necessary for food poisining.

But even when we suspect food poisoning we don't usually do anything special. Dietary management is usually the main treatment. The symptoms are usually the same as for viral illnesses, and we treat them the same way. Sometimes food poisoning does hit kids harder than viral illnesses do. The vomiting can be more frequent, and thus the risk of dehydration more present. But in any case we still treat the symptoms. If the symptoms are more severe, we treat them more aggressively.

Sometimes children will come down with cases of vomiting or diarrhea that at first appear to be caused by a stomach virus, or by food poisoning. Parents may suspect food poisoning at first, because the episodes often occur soon after eating. If this becomes a pattern however, we begin to suspect **food allergies or food intolerance.** Parents will notice that the vomiting and diarrhea happen every time their child eats tomatoes, or strawberries, for example. The episodes of diarrhea and vomiting usually follow the meal pretty quickly, and go away just as quickly.

Parents will often suspect the food at first. "She's eaten bad shrimp," the parents will call and say, after that nice meal of shrimp sub gum at the family's favorite Chinese restaurant. But when it happens again, they realize they can't blame the cook—or the shrimp. It's an allergy. Shellfish, in fact, is a common culprit. So are tomatoes, and many kinds of berries. Allergies to nuts are very common, and even such common foods as peanuts and peanut butter may cause diarrhea and vomiting.

Food allergies and food intolerances sound as if they are the same, but they really aren't. Food intolerance is basically just what it sounds like. Something about the food doesn't agree with the child's body. He can't tolerate it. A major symptom in a food intolerance is vomiting.

An allergy is a more complex reaction, representing the reaction of the child's entire system to the offending food. An allergy can be much more serious than an intolerance. With food allergies, the vomiting isn't necessarily the only or even the major symptom. Instead, we look to see if the vomiting is accompanied by hives or swelling, especially around the mouth, or generalized rashes. The combination of these symptoms can mean a very serious problem. In some cases, allergic children can have throat swelling severe enough to cause breathing difficulties. In extreme cases, as we discuss in our chapter on skin and rashes, the child can go into shock. This kind of food allergy is potentially a very serious condition, and should be taken seriously.

Aside from the obvious gastrointestinal problems, there are a whole range of other possible causes for vomiting. One of them, surprisingly, is **strep throat.** I've seen many children in my practice whose parents brought them to me not chiefly because of a sore throat, but with complaints of fever and vomiting. I've seen kids vomiting so persistently that they need to be sent to the emergency room for intravenous fluids. There we discovered in the course of the routine examination and a throat culture that they had strep throat.

Although it isn't the most prominent symptom, vomiting can also accompany **appendicitis.** In fact, in some stages, gastroenteritis and appendicitis can seem very similar, with stomach pain, a low fever (or no fever) and vomiting. Usually, however, the symptom in appendicitis that parents will find most striking is not the vomiting, but the pain, which builds slowly and consistently in one part of the abdomen. Please look at the chapter on pain if you suspect your child may have appendicitis. It is a serious condition that requires prompt medical attention. But please be reassured, the chances are that vomiting, a low fever and generalized stomach pain are caused by nothing more than the flu.

Kids also vomit for a whole lot of reasons that aren't associated with any specific illness or condition. Vomiting associated with **coughing** is fairly common. Sometimes the child will gag on mucus draining down the back of her throat when she has a bad cold. Sometimes they will swallow enough mucus that it irritates the stomach, causing vomiting. Sometimes the cough itself simply trig-

gers the gag reflex, causing them to gag and then to vomit. In young
children, the gag reflex is so sensitive that they may vomit any time
they get a severe cough. So if your child has a head cold, is coughing
and then suddenly gags and vomits, you don't necessarily need to
worry that she's caught a stomach flu on top of all that. Watch the
circumstances of the vomiting carefully and you may be able to
conclude that the cough itself is to blame.

THE EMOTIONS

Kids' emotions are complex, and they often lack the language
and maturity to cope with them. They also cause a wide range of
physical symptoms. **Anxiety** and stress can make a kid throw up.
If the anxiety is severe enough, or the child is sensitive enough, the
physical symptoms can be quite acute. Kids can get rapid heart
rate, hyperventilate or they can even faint. But stomach aches are
a common symptom, and may even lead to vomiting.

Because the problem may occur predictably every day just before some dreaded event (like going off to school), it's tempting for
adults to attribute more adult motivations to children. Some people
might want to say for example that the child is trying to "get out
of" going to school. It doesn't work like that, though. The child's
anxieties are real. The solution is to try to work with the situation,
not just the symptom. Very often you will find that something has
happened that needs to be addressed, especially if the pain at school
time came on suddenly. Perhaps a teacher is being too strict on an
overly sensitive child; another child may be terrorizing her; some
classmate may have told her there are alligators in the toilets at
school. Whatever it is, it needs to be explored and addressed, by
the parent or if necessary, a professional.

Similarly, kids can vomit from over-exertion. Children under
three years old are especially susceptible. A long hot day at the state
fair in the heat, irregular meals, a ride on the carousel and an over-
stimulating puppet show, and you are setting the stage for having
to hose down the backseat of the car when you get home.

And speaking of cars, some kids vomit simply from **motion**

sickness. Some kids are far more susceptible than others, and will vomit on airplanes, buses, or during even short car rides. Some kids, you will find, never get sick under any circumstances, while some will vomit after a long ride or while reading in a stuffy car. If you know your child is vulnerable, I suggest a dose of Benadryl or Dramamine before the car, plane, train or boat trip. It's the same Benadryl that you might give to your child who was suffering from a stuffy nose, cough or post-nasal drip. That's because Benadryl is an antihistamine, which works very well against kids' motion sickness. You might also want to keep an airsickness bag in your glove compartment.

VOMITING WITH HEADACHES

When a child has an intestinal flu, her vomiting will often be accompanied by fever, a headache and body aches. This is where diagnosing becomes tricky, and where I would advise parents to seek their doctor's advice promptly. For although 99.9 times out of 100, a fever, headache, vomiting and muscle aches signify nothing more than a viral illness, it's that one rare case that we need to watch out for; that combination of symptoms can also mean **meningitis.** As we discussed in the "Fever" chapter, meningitis is a very serious viral or bacterial illness that can be fatal. So even if we are virtually certain that we are dealing with nothing more serious than the flu, I feel many times we have no choice but to take a look at the child.

There are some pretty reliable tests we can do over the phone. The first thing I will do is to have the parent ask the child to get up and walk across the room. Then I'll ask the parent to have her touch her chin to her chest. Those are two pretty reliable signs. Because meningitis infects the spinal fluid, a child with meningitis is going to feel very sick, and certainly not up to walking. What's more the stiff neck that is characteristic of meningitis is quite different from ordinary muscle aches. Again, because it originates from the infection of the spinal fluid, the stiff neck that accompanies meningitis makes it difficult to move the head up and down. Read the chapter on fever for more information, and try the chin-touch test yourself.

Even if your child passes the test, with this combination of symptoms I would strongly urge you to consult your physician, at least by phone.

It may surprise adults to realize that kids who vomit and have bad headaches may be suffering from **migraine.** Even infants get migraine headaches. Usually we are helped in diagnosing migraine by a family history, since it tends to run in families.

A child with migraine will behave much like an adult. She will appear pale, develop a bad headache, and vomit. She may also complain about smells, or sounds or appear sensitive to light.

With children as with adults, migraine often appears to be associated with certain foods, chocolate in particular. If you notice that your child develops migraines and vomits after your regular Baskin-Robbins run, or after birthday parties, or after some friend shares her M&M's, suspect the chocolate. Sometimes it's the combination of chocolate and exertion, like having a Mars Bar before a soccer game. Other possible culprits are vanilla, nuts, and aged cheeses, like cheddar. In this case, once we diagnose the problem, the treatment is simple: BAN the offending food.

Some children may vomit after a **head injury.** Because vomiting after any kind of blow to the head can mean serious injury like a concussion, I suggest you consult your physician promptly. I don't usually get too concerned, however, by a single episode of vomiting after a head injury. As I said earlier, children are so sensitive to stress and trauma that the one vomiting episode can simply be the result of the fall, or of the crying that follows.

The vomiting that concerns me following a head injury is recurrent vomiting. I'll let her throw up once. If she throws up twice, I want to see her. I'll want to check carefully, since recurrent vomiting after a head injury may be a sign of bleeding inside the skull which may be putting pressure on the brain.

Sometimes parents are concerned about **brain tumors** when their children have headaches and complain of vomiting. If you have real concerns, certainly you should see your doctor. But he or she will probably tell you what I would: There is vomiting associated with brain tumors, but not as one of the first symptoms. You would already have been concerned about other things like changes in the child's behavior, staggering, dizziness, or complaints about double vision. These result from pressure building up in the brain, and are apparent long before the pressure gets great enough to lead to vomiting.

YOUR CHILD UNDER SIX MONTHS

You should call your doctor right away for any vomiting in a newborn baby. That's because vomiting in a brand new baby can be a sign of serious illness. But first, let me define vomiting. For anxious, first-time parents, it may take some time to figure out the difference. In the meantime, by all means call the doctor and reassure yourself. But the fact is, in very young babies we need to distinguish between actual vomiting and spitting up, because little babies do a whole lot of spitting up.

Spitting up is the kind of mild, almost matter-of-fact regurgitation that takes place on your shoulder when you are burping her, or maybe even while she is feeding, or when you change her position from lying to sitting up. A little baby's stomach can only hold so much. If she's over-fed, the stomach will distend and then contract to push the food down into the intestine. The problem is, some of it comes out the other end instead. A baby will also spit up while trying to expel air she took in during feeding, or from an abrupt change in position.

Vomiting is different. It is more forceful. The vomit doesn't just drizzle out down the chin, but shoots out, beyond the baby's face and clothing. When we find a newborn truly vomiting, we take it seriously.

One thing we will check for is an **intestinal obstruction.** The younger the baby is, the more we tend to think of anatomical abnormalities. After a month, or six weeks of age, we begin to think more of other causes.

Just last year I treated a child with an intestinal obstruction. This baby had vomited easily from the time she was born. Her mother had to feed her very slowly and carefully to get her to keep anything down. She had vomited both on breast milk and on formula. The problem really became severe when she got old enough to start on solid food. Everything solid her parents fed her came back up sooner or later. When we x-rayed the baby, we found that she had a stomach that tapered down to a pin-sized opening before reaching her lower intestines. Liquid could get through—slowly—but not solids.

This baby's obstruction was high up in the digestive system. We would have been even more suspicious if the obstruction had been lower down. That could have caused her vomit to have a yellow or greenish color to it. The yellow color is from bile fluid being vomited up. This could be a surgical problem that needs to be addressed quickly, so consult your doctor right away.

One other clue should have been the fact that this baby regularly vomited up breast milk. Babies usually tolerate breast milk very well. A baby who vomits breast milk regularly has some more serious condition, like a severe **allergy** or some kind of obstruction, and should be looked at promptly.

Problems with formula are common. Another common cause of vomiting in young babies is **milk intolerance** or **milk allergy.** A baby who isn't being breast fed may be allergic to the milk-based formulas that most parents choose instead. Intolerance to cow's milk is also not uncommon, and the treatment for either will be a change to a soy-based preparation or a formula like Nutramigen.

Some babies who are breast feeding can react with either colic or vomiting to milk or cheese that the mother has eaten. In that case, we take the mother herself off cow milk products, to eliminate the offending protein.

In infants, we also consider gastroenteritis as a cause of vomiting, especially if there are older siblings in the house.

There is another type of vomiting that we see in very young children, vomiting that is much more vigorous than spitting up or ordinary vomiting. This is **projectile vomiting.** Projectile vomiting can be quite dramatic. The contents of the stomach expel from the baby with quite some force—enough to shoot it out across a room, to a distance of five feet or more. Usually it occurs within the first few weeks of life without fever or any other symptoms.

Projectile vomiting is a sign of a condition known as **pyloric**

stenosis, a narrowing of the pyloric valve. That's the valve between the stomach and the small intestines. This condition requires a surgical correction that, although simple, must be done promptly.

Frequent vomiting, on the other hand, may be caused by **gastro-esophogeal reflux.** All that means is that the valve at the top of the stomach isn't yet completely formed. That's the valve that keeps food down in the stomach while the digestive system does its work. Vomiting from this cause can be severe enough that it interferes with the child's growth. A child can't grow, after all, if all his nourishment is winding up on the carpet. Usually, however, this type of vomiting, while a nuisance, isn't serious, and is quickly outgrown.

With very young babies, we need to be particularly concerned about **dehydration.** With babies under two months, you should call your doctor for any vomiting at all. Even for babies up to six months of age, a call to the doctor is in order. Babies just don't have as much mass as older kids, so they can lose needed fluids much more quickly. The younger they are, the more concerned I am. I would worry more about a two-month-old than a four-month-old, more about a four-month-old than a six-month-old. Body weight plays a role too: A chubby, hearty two-month-old is a completely different creature from a tiny four-month-old who was born prematurely.

Watch your baby's behavior. Call the doctor immediately for any child whose crying becomes weak or stops, or who becomes lethargic and seems apathetic.

CHECKLIST

VOMITING WITH DIARRHEA AND FEVER: Consider stomach flu.

VOMITING WITH HIGH FEVER: Call the doctor. This could be a symptom of a whole range of serious illnesses, like meningitis, strep throat or a serious bacterial infection.

VOMITING WITH A SORE THROAT: Consider strep throat.

VOMITING AFTER EATING WITH NO FEVER: Consider food intolerance or allergy.

VOMITING WITH RASH, HIVES, OR SWELLING AFTER EATING: Consider food allergies.

STOMACH ACHE OR VOMITING AT REGULAR TIMES, OR BEFORE CERTAIN EVENTS: Consider anxiety.

VOMITING IN THE CAR, PLANE OR BOAT: Consider motion sickness.

VOMITING WITH SEVERE HEADACHE, NO FEVER: Consider migraine.

TREATMENT

You treat vomiting just as you do diarrhea: liquids to prevent dehydration, dietary management to ease the child out of the effects of the virus.

Remember that a child who is vomiting, even from a common virus, is a child with a very sensitive stomach. Liquids should be given in small amounts, lest they come right back up again. Try the same liquids I suggest for diarrhea: flat Coke or ginger ale, an electrolyte solution like Pedialyte, diluted apple juice, or plain water. Avoid any food if possible for the first 24 hours of the vomiting attack. Eating solids sooner may just prolong the irritation which in turn will prolong the vomiting.

If you find that your child immediately throws up anything he eats or drinks, or that whatever he drinks goes right through him, then you need to take special measures. His stomach is too irritated to tolerate anything in volume, and his irritated intestines are just passing things through as quickly as they go in. Usually such hypersensitivity only lasts for a few hours. But for those few hours, the child needs to get some liquid to replace what is being lost. The trick, then, is to get the fluids into him in small, steady quantities.

Most doctors in this case recommend ice chips. These work just fine. Even if your child sucks on a small quantity of ice chips over an afternoon, he will probably be getting enough liquid to stave off dehydration. The only problem with ice chips is that—like electrolyte solutions—it's often difficult to get kids to eat them.

I find popsicles an elegant solution. By popsicles, I don't mean the ice cream type, but the ones that are made mostly of water. Try some of the popular all fruit juice brands if you object to giving your child too much sugar or food coloring. Or make your own. Some parents keep small popsicle molds around for just such an occasion. For some reason even sick kids will happily devour a quantity of juice—if it's *frozen*—that they wouldn't tolerate if they were simply handed it in a glass. If your child eats a popsicle or two, it's the same as a cup of juice, and probably enough to hold him till he can take more substantial things.

SHALL I WAKE THE DOCTOR?

Wake the doctor if your child has:

- ❖ A combination of vomiting and a high fever—say, over 104 degrees.
- ❖ Vomiting in conjunction with severe, persistent, abdominal pain.
- ❖ Vomiting with hives, swelling, itching—especially around the mouth.
- ❖ Persistent vomiting with lethargy, a weak cry and dry mouth. Wake your doctor if your baby under two months old has persistent vomiting (more than one or two episodes in an hour or two).

CAN SHE GO BACK TO SCHOOL?

With a viral illness, or food poisoning, it's usually safe to send a child back to school 24 hours after the fever has returned to normal, and after the last episode of vomiting, presuming that the child appears comfortable enough to do so.

With migraine, the child herself will give you the clue. Send her back when she appears well enough and comfortable enough to do so.

With vomiting associated with anxiety, you will need to do some serious analysis of the situation to find out what is causing the emotional distress. It doesn't make any sense to keep sending a child back into a classroom where she is stressed enough to cause vomiting without figuring out how to take steps to alleviate whatever it is that is causing the anxiety.

ASK DR. JOHN

QUESTION: My two-year-old seems to vomit at the drop of a hat. His four-year-old brother never seemed to vomit at all. Why?

ANSWER: Vomiting, like many other conditions, is very particular. Just as one child always runs a high fever, or seems especially prone to ear infections, some children just seem to have tummies that are very sensitive.

NOTES

NOTES

NOTES

NOTES

NOTES

NOTES

NOTES

NOTES